How to be a
TEAM LEADER

hamlyn

How to be a
TEAM LEADER

THE SIMPLE WAY TO BUILD AND MANAGE AN EFFECTIVE TEAM

David Simmonds

**This book is dedicated to the Leadership Team
at Lewin (www.lewin.org.uk), who give so generously
of themselves and their time, and from whom I've
learned so much.**

First published in Great Britain in 2004 by
Hamlyn, a division of Octopus Publishing Group Ltd
2–4 Heron Quays, London E14 4JP

ISBN 0 600 60960 X

A CIP catalogue record for this book is available
from the British Library

Printed and bound in China

10 9 8 7 6 5 4 3 2 1

CONTENTS

INTRODUCTION

Teamwork and leadership are obviously closely linked and they are vital to the health and continuing success of any organization. If you are new to teamwork, and in particular if you are new to leadership, then this is the book for you.

About this book

This book is based on the best research available and has been specially designed to be instantly accessible. Of course you can read it straight through from cover to cover, but you can just as easily dip in to find the particular sections that are of relevance to your current situation. Whichever approach you choose, the book will tell you all you need to know about team leadership in a fun way.

You will find lots of short, snappy sections full of easy-to-remember tips and hints. The pictures and diagrams add interest and will also help you to retain what you have learned. There are plenty of enjoyable exercises for you to complete as well.

To get the most out of this book, mark the passages that you find especially interesting or useful and then make a point of discussing them with other people.

'Once you start working together effectively, you'll find that 2 and 2 really can make 5!'

Where to begin?

Team leadership is an enormous subject and one that's growing all the time. The existing literature already fills many library shelves, so you could spend the rest of your life trying to read it all!

The answer is to be realistic. There is no way that you are going to be able to learn everything immediately, so just try one new thing at a time. Experiment with a new idea or skill and see how you get on. You will make mistakes – that's only natural – but your aim should be to learn from them.

It is very important to find yourself a mentor – someone who will help you, look after you and assist you in your career. Talk to them regularly about what you are learning and about how you are trying to put it into practice.

DO

- **Rely on your team**
- **Seek help from others**
- **Try out new ways of doing things**
- **Have fun**

DON'T

- **Try to have all the answers**
- **Try to do everyone else's job**
- **Try to be an expert at everything**
- **Try to be the best leader in the world**

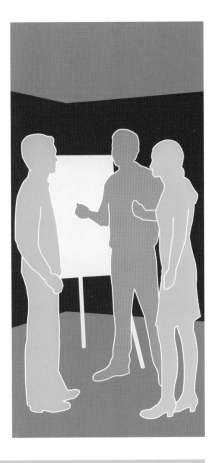

1 YOUR TEAM

Putting your team together could be one of the most difficult – and rewarding – tasks you face as a leader.

CREATING YOUR TEAM

FIRST STEPS

- **Don't rush**
- **Don't pretend**
- **Don't try too hard**

So, you're going to be leading a team. Perhaps you've just been promoted to head up an existing group that you've been part of for a long time. Or you've been offered the job of leading a team in a different department or even a new organization. Or you've simply decided to form a brand-new team. This is a golden opportunity for you to grasp with both hands.

Some people will feel daunted by the thought of all the new responsibilities that lie ahead, while others will immediately relish the challenge. How you react obviously depends on a range of different factors. Remember, though, that working in a team, with a team, for a team and as part of a team can be one of the most rewarding parts of modern business life. And if you are able to help that team reach its objectives as a result of your effective leadership, this will be one of the most enriching aspects of your whole career.

When people stop working on their own and come together, united in a common purpose, then magical things can happen! You will find that you are able to accomplish far more, and do so more effectively, when you act collectively to achieve your goals.

Teamworking

Do not make the mistake of thinking that teamworking is something that just happens magically. You are going to have to make it work. As a new team leader, it will be your responsibility to create your team. So, the first thing you need to do is look at ways of blending together the individuals who make up the working group in order to form an efficient and effective unit.

Do teams work?

From the beginning of the twentieth century, with Western economies relying on heavy industry and large manufacturing plants, owners insisted upon employees producing greater quantities of goods for lower costs. Time and motion studies were conducted with a view to increasing efficiency. In the automobile industry – Ford with its production line is the famous example – jobs were analysed in minute detail and broken down into individual tasks, with each worker undertaking just one part of the production process.

By the 1970s, however, with the coming of new technology, managers could see that this approach was no longer viable. Workers could not carry on indefinitely making more and more. Western economies were also becoming increasingly based on the service sector. For all these reasons, managers needed to develop new ways of working, supported by other means of achieving better results. Autonomous work groups provided the answer. To take car manufacturing as an example again – Volvo in this particular case – a small team of workers would now build a whole car together. The company then found not only that the team produced more cars over time, but also that those cars were of excellent quality.

Help! I can't do it on my own. We need to do this together.

We all feel sometimes that if only other people at work would leave us alone for a while, we could plan our time constructively, decide on our long-term priorities and set our immediate goals.

BUILDING RELATIONSHIPS

Pulling together

Unfortunately, work just isn't like that. Even self-employed artists painting alone in their studios need other people. They need to be supported by family and friends through the difficult times; they need suppliers to provide their canvas, paint and brushes; and they need agents or a gallery or two to sell their pictures.

As those of our colleagues in logistics know only too well, we're all part of a long chain of individuals, departments and organizations that depend on each other. Or, to use another image, you may prefer to see your job as an essential element in a network – or web – of mutually dependent parts. Some writers have described modern working practices as being a bit like an ecosystem, where each component is important in sustaining and developing the whole.

Basically, we all need help. We can't do everything on our own, no matter how tempted we might sometimes be to try!

As a team leader, you need the people in your team to help you do your job – and they definitely need you to help them do theirs. And you will find, as you work together, not only that you can do more, but also that you can do it better.

Two heads are better than one

Coming together at work is a deliberate social activity with which some people are going to feel more comfortable than others. Leaving aside for the moment various problems to do with different cultural norms, how we relate in teams is very important. We need to get near to those around us.

We all have different strengths and weaknesses. Your job as leader will be to help your team to identify these and acknowledge them. It is your responsibility to encourage people to come together, to relate together and to work together. In many ways, this will be the most difficult task for you to accomplish!

'Individual commitment to a group effort – that is what makes a team work, a company work, a society work, a civilization work.'

– *Vince Lombardi*

PUTTING IT INTO PRACTICE
- **Meet regularly**
- **Communicate freely**
- **Listen actively**

We can all benefit from being in a closer working relationship with the people around us. That is not to say that everyone should become the best of friends — far from it!

BUILDING TRUST

But over the years research has consistently shown that the better we are at understanding the needs and aspirations of our colleagues, the better we are able to do our own jobs.

How to make a start

As a leader, you must strive to include each and every member of your team. Obviously, not everyone is going to have the same kind of relationship with all the team members. Different people will relate in different ways with other individuals, depending on the circumstances at the time.

The rainbow

Here's something to try in the workplace. It's easy to carry out and is good fun, particularly after lunch on a Friday afternoon!

Imagine your team as the colours in the rainbow. Red, orange, yellow, green, blue, indigo and violet — all of them are needed. Get team members to choose a different colour and then say how they feel about belonging and contributing to the whole rainbow.

For example, if nobody else has selected it first, I might choose 'blue'. This is not only my favourite colour, but I think it reflects something of my personality. Being the colour of the sky and the sea, it seems to indicate vast horizons and endless possibilities. I like to dream big dreams. However, in a team, I know we need other 'colours' too. There will be those, maybe 'green' for example, who have their feet firmly on the ground, who will turn those dreams into realities. Another person, say 'yellow', often brings light, life and happiness to the team ... and so on. You can think of other meanings for the colours.

Encourage loyalty

At all times, your job is to make sure that everyone's contribution is recognized and employed for the good of the team. Nobody should be excluded or ignored. You will then find that individual productivity is enhanced, as well as the quality of the whole team's output.

One of the best things you can do as a leader is to encourage a sense of loyalty and commitment. People need to fit in. As members of the team develop that sense of belonging, they will unconsciously start to think of themselves collectively, using phrases such as 'We did a good job with that tender submission' or 'Our office is looking really bright these days.' In other words, they will start pulling in the same direction, focusing on shared goals.

Ownership of joint aims will inspire team members to want to work not just for themselves but also for each other. They will want to protect the team and its resources. People will develop a sense of urgency, while friendly competition with other teams will increase their common purpose.

'A certain awkwardness marks the use of borrowed thoughts; but as soon as we have learned what to do with them, they become our own.' – *Ralph Waldo Emerson*

PUTTING IT INTO PRACTICE

- **Embrace diversity**
- **Be inclusive**
- **Give respect**

Getting results is normally all that senior managers worry about. This tends to be because most organizations set targets in purely financial terms.

BUILDING COMMITMENT

'The nice thing about teamwork is that you always have others on your side.'

– Margaret Carty

Quantitative measures alone are used to assess the efficiency of particular departments, business units and individuals. However, this should not deter you from your emphasis on good teamwork, because that is the best way to meet your targets effectively.

Communication is the key

Some writers have insisted that everyone at work has a drive to achieve – an instinctive desire, if you like, to accomplish objectives and attain higher goals. Well, this may be true of many people, but do not automatically assume that it holds for everyone. If you find this is the case, you will need to work out what else fires them.

You could always do worse than ask them! Why not sit down with each member of the team on their own for just 15 minutes or so. A coffee or fruit juice usually helps to dispel any nerves. After the normal pleasantries, steer the conversation round to asking something like, 'What makes you stay late at work?' or 'Why did you put in that extra effort preparing for the meeting?'

PUTTING IT INTO PRACTICE

- Encourage creativity
- Explore boundaries
- Celebrate successes

KEY RESULTS AREAS

Step 1

It is essential for you to set out the requirements of your own job. To do this, it is important first of all to clarify the purpose of what you do and the key results areas. In just one sentence, write down the *overall purpose* of the job in the central oblong box below.

Step 2

Then identify the six most important *key results areas* of your work and write them in the oval spaces.

Step 3

Now ask your team members to do this for themselves.

Step 4

Finally, get them to do it on each other's jobs – including yours! Find some quality time – at least an hour or two – to have a good discussion about what you have all discovered.

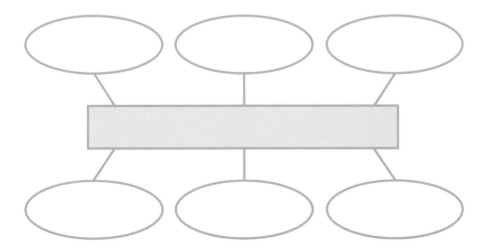

More is constantly being demanded of those at work. But what does 'more' actually mean? And how is it measured?

BUILDING SUCCESS

'Measuring more is easy. Measuring better is hard.'

– *Charles Handy*

PUTTING IT INTO PRACTICE

- Monitor goals
- Improve constantly
- Review task and process

Answering difficult questions

Your team will look to you for help with questions such as these. The answers are not always easy to find, but it is important for all of you to grapple with the difficulties until you reach a solution. Only then will you be in a position to move forward.

When it comes to performance management, you will need to take a long, hard look at where you are now before going on to ask where you want to be. And it is absolutely vital not to impose your views on others, but to get the whole team involved from the start. In other words, ask them – don't tell them!

Most appraisal arrangements or competence schemes have been developed on this basis. Make sure that there are opportunities for your team members to assess their own performance first. Only then can you have a meaningful discussion.

After that, you could involve the others as well. This is known in many organizations as 'peer assessment'.

Once the team feels comfortable with this, then you can develop all-round evaluation, called '360° feedback'. To give and receive this kind of feedback will require considerable trust, openness and honesty. Your job is to encourage such transparency in all your relationships.

Each person needs to identify those they associate mostly closely with in the course of their work, including individuals both inside and outside the organization. This is called 'stakeholder analysis'.

Ask each member of your team to carry out this sort of an analysis and then sit down together to compare your results.

What are the similarities? What are the differences?
Later, we will discuss how you can obtain feedback
from these stakeholders to help you to improve
performance.

360° FEEDBACK

Who do you relate to at work? Put some names against
each of the categories below. You can add your own
categories as well.

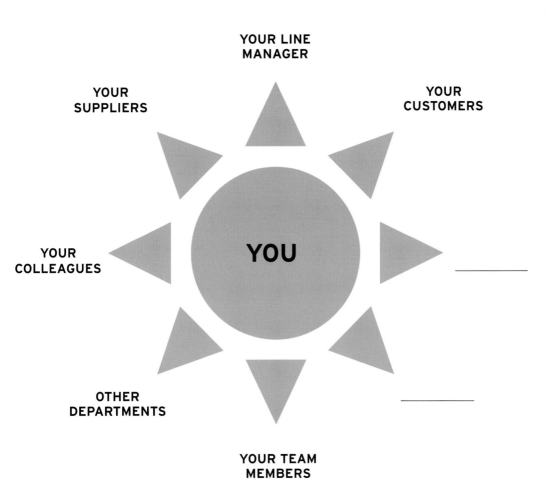

YOUR LINE
MANAGER

YOUR
SUPPLIERS

YOUR
CUSTOMERS

YOUR
COLLEAGUES

YOU

_____

OTHER
DEPARTMENTS

_____

YOUR TEAM
MEMBERS

As we have seen, we can do far more working with each other than when we're struggling on our own. There are two key elements here: effort and direction.

PULLING TOGETHER

Effort

As a team leader, you must encourage every member of your team to play a full part in the overall performance of the team. As each individual makes a deliberate effort to do his or her best, so the team's accomplishments will increase. Now, none of us can work at peak performance all the time – and if we try, then we'll soon be burnt out! But as a team we can help to share the load and ease the burden. Then, when there is an important rush job or a tight deadline to meet, team players will find they want to help one another to meet those goals.

Increasingly, those with responsibility in organizations are developing this new method of directing the work of their teams. It is known as 'servant leadership' and, as you demonstrate the approach in your everyday work life, so your team members will imitate and follow your example. The old-fashioned 'command and control' management style is now looking more and more obsolete. Instead, what you need to do is to encourage, enable and facilitate those around you to fulfil their potential and enhance their performance.

Direction

It is essential to recognize here that we are not talking about you directing your people. Many managers still attempt to impose their will on subordinates and insist that they obey orders. That, however, is ultimately a very short-term strategy, as these days most employees are likely to leave the organization rather than put up with such bullying.

THE THREE MEASURES OF QUALITY AND SUCCESS

1 Completeness

2 Accuracy

3 Promptness

Instead, we are discussing the need to provide your people with vision and purpose. Then they will be able to contribute towards the team goals. Your role is to supply that direction. Now, you won't be able to do that in isolation from the teams around you with which you work. Inevitably, you must take account of departmental and organizational strategies.

Your team will expect you to give them a strong lead with regard to its course over the short, the medium and the long term. So, in conjunction with your own manager and head of department, you must establish:

• The route you will follow
• The goals you will accomplish
• The methods you will adopt
• The resources you will need

GIVING DIRECTION

• **The compass**
  Which way do we go?

• **The map**
  What's our plan?

• **The binoculars**
  What is the vision?

• **The rope**
  What values do we hold on to?

PUTTING IT INTO PRACTICE

• **Ask for help**

• **Offer support**

• **Contribute freely**

Organizing a team is never going to be easy, but it will certainly be one of your most important jobs.

GATHERING RESOURCES

You're dealing with people, not machines

If there's one thing people don't like, it's thinking that they're being pushed around. They may not say anything to you directly, but once you're out of earshot, they will grumble and moan about you and the demands you've placed upon them.

Remember, the members of your team have feelings, opinions and memories – just like you! So, your overriding principle should be to include, consult and respect them, both individually and collectively. Get them involved right from the beginning. Their collective knowledge, skills and experience will always be far greater than yours, so the way forward is obvious – use them! As a result, your decisions, actions and outcomes can only be better.

Apart from anything else, by drawing your group in, they will become more committed – to you, to your joint decisions and to each other. The ensuing mutual trust and loyalty are precious commodities and you must do all you can to foster them. Remember, once such trust is betrayed, it will be much harder to regain it.

Beware 'group think'

In addition to the people in your own team, there could well be other people in other teams within your organization. Don't be tempted to think that yours is the only team that counts. Nor should you imagine that your team is the best – even if you do consistently win all the office competitions! If you find your mind wandering in that direction, be careful: you are in danger of falling into the group-think trap. This is not a useful place to be, as you're basically saying, 'We're the best simply because we say so!'

Some teams, groups and organizations – not to mention nations – have come to blows for this very reason. As a result, they have become very vulnerable, leaving themselves open to attack from competitors. Meanwhile, others have forged ahead by keeping a weather eye out for changes in the environment and the external context.

Therefore, in order to be able to respond appropriately to the many forces for change that exist, it is essential for you to make a realistic assessment of your team's strengths and weaknesses.

WHAT EVERY TEAM NEEDS

A GATEKEEPER – who welcomes people from the outside into the team and encourages team members to explore elsewhere.

AN OBSERVER – who watches carefully what is happening on the horizons surrounding the team and also sees what the team is doing.

PUTTING IT INTO PRACTICE

- Discover what's available
- Determine what's feasible
- Decide what's a priority

Good relationships are obviously central to teamwork. Everyone needs to know where they fit in and how they relate to those around them.

SHARING AND CARING

How to turn theory into practice

Many organizations invest huge sums of money in 'team-building' events. These can range from outdoor development courses, including caving, climbing and camping, to simulated activities such as having to get the team across a 'shark-infested chasm' in a field by just using a few barrels and planks!

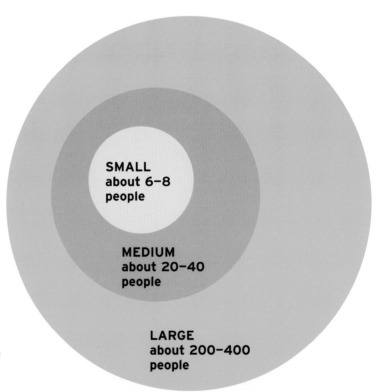

SMALL
about 6–8
people

MEDIUM
about 20–40
people

Research suggests that we all need to belong to three different-sized groups. Try to identify three different-sized groups that you belong to.

LARGE
about 200–400
people

Such organizations have obviously acknowledged the potential benefits of events like these to encourage greater understanding and trust between team members. Unfortunately, the facilitators of the activities often lack the necessary skills to debrief the participants and to encourage the transfer of learning back into the workplace.

To foster that sense of belonging in your team, you will need to develop an awareness of one another's needs. This will include an understanding of the pressures and tensions that can build up and oppress everyone at work at one time or another, and perhaps also sensitivity to the pressures and difficulties of sustaining a fulfilling home life.

PUTTING IT INTO PRACTICE

- **Reach out to one another**
- **Support one another**
- **Consider one another**

Counselling

If any members of your team are experiencing problems – whether at home or at work – that are affecting their work, then it is your right and responsibility to offer help and support. Naturally, you cannot insist that they accept your offer, and you certainly must not try to take their problems away from them – you've got enough of your own! But you must explore with them ways they can solve their own difficulties. This is known as counselling.

Don't imagine that you have to immediately become an amateur psychiatrist when counselling, but you do need to develop two basic skills: to ask questions and to listen to the answers.

ASK QUESTIONS

- **Closed**
- **Open**
- **Probe**
- **Summarize**

LISTEN TO THE ANSWERS

- **Look interested**
- **Inspire confidence**
- **Seek clarification**
- **Test understanding**
- **Enquire sensitively**
- **Neutralize emotions**

Knowledge workers are increasingly becoming the backbone of many organizations. In fact, it has been said that they are the most valuable assets of most organizations.

CONTRIBUTING UNDERSTANDING

What do you know?

Knowledge management is all about harnessing these precious assets. For you as a team leader, this means you must do all you can to help your people to share their knowledge.

While a number of experts stress the need for ever more efficient electronic portals, databases and intranets, your task as a knowledge manager is to encourage your team to bring into the open what is currently locked in their brains. Some writers have described this as a process of changing tacit knowledge into explicit knowledge.

One way to begin to explore how well you contribute to sharing knowledge at work is to construct a knowledge map. This is a simple graphical representation of how you operate, both individually and/or as a team.

A knowledge map identifies all internal and external stakeholders for a particular task or project – strategic partners, suppliers, customers, and so on – and illustrates the complex ways in which participants work together. It shows how people can add three different kinds of value:

1 Tangible benefits – goods, services, money etc.
2 Intangible benefits – brand, loyalty, respect etc.
3 Knowledge – strategic information, planning, processes etc.

You can do this for yourself, another team member, or the whole team together.

The ways in which we inhabit the spaces between us, will in future determine the nature of our work.

KNOWLEDGE MAPPING

This is a visual representation of business relationships showing the flow of knowledge.

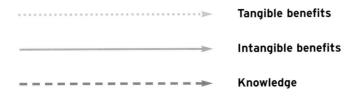

Tangible benefits

Intangible benefits

Knowledge

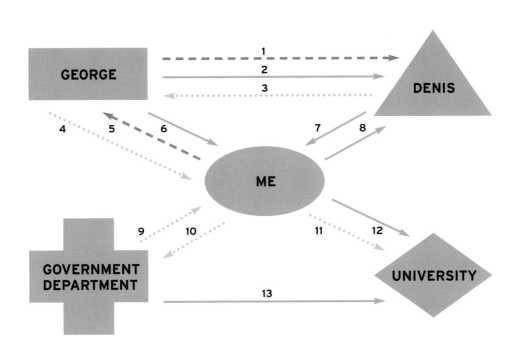

In the knowledge mapping example on the previous page, George (the Managing Director of the client organization) wants me (working as a consultant for a University) to produce a marketing plan for him. My colleague Denis has known George for some years, and they have shared a great deal together over that time. Additional finance is also available from a Government Department.

1 and 3: George and Denis give each other strategic information

2 and 6: George gives Denis and me respect

4 and 9: George and the Government Department give me money

5: I give George a marketing plan

7 and 8: Denis and I share loyalty

10 and 11: I give the Government Department and the University a report

12 and 13: The Government Department and I give the University enhanced image

It is useful to ask the other key players on occasion to construct a similar knowledge map – and then to compare the outcomes.

PUTTING IT INTO PRACTICE

- **Give freely**
- **Be curious**
- **Ask, 'Why not?'**

Change and leadership

In most Westernized economies, senior managers are now recognizing that their knowledge workers make a vital contribution to both the growth and the sustainability of their organizations.

So, there are obviously close bonds between learning, change and knowledge. Leadership binds these different areas together by fostering interpersonal relationships, by knowledge working and by its focus on others.

Knowledge and leadership

The diagram below shows another way of looking at knowledge work and its links with leadership.

For leadership to be effective it must encompass eight separate but interrelated features. You can see how each of these factors are important to the 'drivewheel' of leadership. None is more important than the other, but all of them are vital to a productive team.

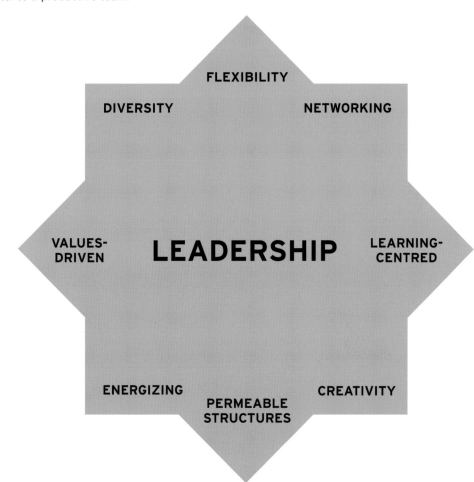

'Management works in the system. Leadership works on the system.' – *Stephen Covey*

Much has been accomplished through equal opportunities legislation over the last 20 years. Overt discrimination has gradually been dealt with in the workplace.

CELEBRATING DIFFERENCES

'Coming together is a beginning, staying together is progress and working together is success.'

– Henry Ford

Management is being forced to consider every aspect of the working life of their employees from different perspectives and to take practical steps to meet the needs of those who have traditionally been in a weakened or impoverished position.

Laws are not enough

Simply changing the law will never change some people's attitudes. At best, they may be made to confront arrogant or condescending behaviour. At worst, they may simply develop a subversive and damaging approach, only barely hidden beneath a thin veneer of 'political correctness'.

The best idea is to educate staff to embrace the notion of diversity. In this way, workers will not be stereotyped into groups and categorized by their external features. They will no longer be patronized by their bosses – usually white middle-class, middle-aged males.

An appreciation of diversity allows you to celebrate people's differences. It is an ongoing process and will enable you to look at others and honestly say, 'You're different from me. That's good! I want you to help me understand you better, because I know I can benefit from what you tell me.'

Assume nothing ... challenge everything

It should no longer be acceptable when recruiting new people to ask on the application form or at the interview about, for example, marital status, age or religious background. You cannot make useful assumptions from answers to questions such as these.

Your team will benefit from having as members people who are different from one another. Cloning is definitely not to be advocated in the business environment! Therefore, you should look at new and different ways of advertising your vacancies. Perhaps you could reflect on job-sharing possibilities or flexible working arrangements. Take time to consider the physical constraints of the area in which your team members have to work and ask yourself how these might affect different people.

Remember that basic science lesson on the enormous power of magnetism: like poles repel, but opposites attract! Go out of your way to find people unlike yourself. Spend time with them. Get to know them as individuals, not as members of any one particular group. Discover as much as possible about them. What makes them tick? What do they value? What is their personal or cultural history? What are their particular likes and dislikes?

Go on from here to broaden your experience by drawing on those things in their lives that you have yet to encounter. Take a risk! Try something different!

We are all individuals and we are all unique. The influences that have helped to create us – in addition to our parents – include a wide range of different factors:

- Family
- Friends
- Housing
- Education
- Money
- Politics
- Religion
- Values
- Geography
- Opportunities

To a certain extent, we behave and think differently depending on those we are with. To put it another way, we are a function of those with whom we interact. Therefore, a close-knit team will have a major influence over its members, their attitudes and their behaviour.

You should be aware that the various members of your team will see you differently and react to you in a variety of different ways.

In addition, they will respond to each other differently. What is important is that a balance is held between the needs of individuals and those of the team.

To help you to become more aware of what is happening with your people, you could analyse verbal behaviour during a team meeting or a briefing session (see pages 34–35).

However, it is not sufficient to identify and analyse specific behaviours in isolation. Successful interaction lies in seeing how different behaviours can combine to produce identifiable styles.

Natural patterns

Certain behaviours tend to be displayed in pairs. For example, people who do a lot of 'Seeking information' are also likely to do a lot of 'Testing understanding'. The same applies to 'Disagreeing' and 'Defending/attacking', and also to 'Supporting' and 'Building'.

Personal patterns

It is important for leaders to be very aware of their own personal behaviour patterns before seeking to help others understand themselves. People who are aggressive ('Defend/attack') and unaware of it are likely to be very frustrated in their working relationships. Conversely, those who perceive themselves as aggressive and yet are not so are likely to be ineffective when it comes to trying to influence others.

Persuasion patterns

Persuasion is increasingly one of the key skills of leaders. As organizations become 'leaner and fitter', so leaders are often called upon to achieve results in collaboration with those over whom they have no direct authority. As leaders change from direct managers to internal facilitators, so they are required to use considerable powers of persuasion.

In order to do this effectively, you need to use a range of verbal behaviours.

ANALYSING VERBAL BEHAVIOUR IN GROUPS

CATEGORY	DEFINITION	EXAMPLES
Proposing	To put forward a new suggestion, proposal or course of action	'Let's deal with that when we come to item 5.'
Giving information	To offer facts, opinions or clarification	'I said that because the lab carried out the tests last week.'
Supporting	To make a conscious and direct declaration of agreement or support	'John is right. That's what we should do.'
Building	To extend or develop another's proposal	'Yes, I agree. And if we costed it in detail, we could present it to the board at next week's meeting.'
Seeking information	To seek facts, opinions or clarification	'Which features of the process do you think would help us most?'
Summarizing	To restate in compact form what has been discussed	'So we're saying, then, that we can go ahead if it's finished by 15 February.'
Disagreeing	To raise obstacles or objections to a suggestion	'That wouldn't work in our department. We tried it last year and it didn't work then either.'
Bringing in	To invite the views or opinions of a participant	'What do you think your people in Marketing should do on this one, John?'
Shutting out	To attempt to exclude a group member from the discussion	'No. I don't care what you say, I'm determined to push this through.'
Defending/ attacking	To deflect the argument away from the issue and on to a person	'That just proves you're either a fool or a liar. What can you expect from Sales!'
Testing understanding	To establish the extent to which a contribution has been understood	'So you think we should buy five more of these books, is that what you're saying?'

Behaviour analysis in groups

Use a form of this type to keep a tally of what your people actually do in a group meeting or team briefing. As this is a time-consuming exercise and will take a lot of concentration, either get someone else to complete it (such as a trainer or a human resources professional) or give the job of chairing the meeting to someone else.

BEHAVIOURS	NAMES				COMMENTS
	DS	DW	MW	CP	
Proposing	III	HH	II	HH HH	
Giving information	III	IIII	II	HH HH	
Supporting	HH HH	III	II	I	
Building	HH HH	III	II	I	
Seeking information	II	HH HH	II	HH HH	
Summarizing		III			
Disagreeing	I	III	IIII	II	
Bringing in	II	IIII	I	II	
Shutting out	I	I	IIII	I	
Defending/ attacking	I	III	HH II	II	
Testing understanding	II	HH HH	II	HH HH	

A sociogram

Another way to record what's happening in the group is to draw arrows every time something is said from the speaker to the person being addressed.

DS seems to mostly make contributions that are 'building' and 'supporting'.

DW on the other hand tends to make a lot of contributions, particularly in the areas of 'seeking information' and 'testing understanding'. He appears to ignore **CP** entirely.

MW by comparison makes fewer contributions, and most of them are negative – 'disagreeing', 'shutting out' and 'defending/ attacking'. He appears to ignore **CP** entirely.

CP however appears to take on more of a facilitator's role, making a large number of contributions, almost exclusively in order to help the group – 'proposing', 'giving and seeking information' and 'testing understanding'. However, all his contributions are directed only at **MW**.

Once such an analysis is seen and shared by the group, it can have a remarkable effect! Usually, most people say 'I didn't think I spoke so much!' or 'Did I really come across as so controlling?' or even 'I wouldn't be that negative in real life.'

After that, the team leader can see how people can be developed. For example, **MW** could be encouraged to go on a 'Listening Skills' course.

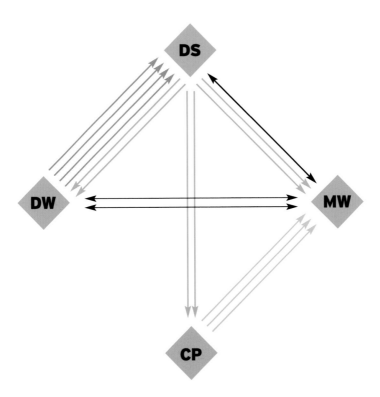

Networking is a way we can work these days to bring about change with and through other people. It is particularly relevant when considering teamwork.

GETTING IT TOGETHER

'Leadership has a harder job to do than just choose sides. It must bring sides together.'

– Jesse Jackson

It's not what you know – it's who you know

This is very true in many areas of life, but it's not the whole truth. Sometimes, it's not who you know, but rather who they know!

Networking is central in establishing good relationships both within the team and with others outside. As a leader, you should set an example for your team members to follow, creating and maintaining contacts with individuals and other teams.

Take the initiative. Be selfless in your efforts to make new friendships and relationships with associates. Be constantly on the lookout for possible new acquaintances. Keep asking people questions about themselves rather than focusing on yourself. By concentrating on their abilities, interests and problems, you will endear yourself to them. By listening to them as individuals, you will demonstrate your interest in them.

As a result, you will be able to find ways to make use of their skills, contacts and interests later. Often, they will offer you opportunities to work together in surprising and exciting ways.

Think of the spider

When a spider is creating its web, it must first let out a long string of fluid from its body and then hang from the end of it. It then rests there, just waiting. It is quite happy to wait until the wind blows it across to a nearby branch. It doesn't struggle or fret or panic. The spider cannot control the breeze but knows that it is necessary to help it do what it cannot do for itself. Once the spider has made contact with the branch, then it is able to spin its web. So it is with us. Once you are secure in your team, you need to build new networks. While there are things you must do as part of that process, some of which only you can accomplish, you must also wait to see which way the wind is blowing. You must expect the unexpected and be watchful for unforeseen encounters. In order to do that, you must allow yourself to move away from the security of your usual environment, the safety of your everyday work and the comfort of routine expectations. The consequence will be that you are able to create something of tremendous beauty!

Once you are free of those constraints, you will find that you come into contact with an amazing array of interesting people and organizations. And they in turn will be able to help and support you in your endeavours thanks to their expertise, abilities and contacts.

- **Be creative**
- **Look for possibilities**
- **Seek opportunities**
- **Expect the unexpected**

Make a point of accepting invitations to meetings, seminars and conferences, especially when you cannot immediately see the connection with your work or your team. There might well be someone there with whom you could establish an excellent working relationship. Also be ready to invite unusual or unknown people to work with you or to meet your team.

Be willing to take your whole team out to a new location. It is often surprising how much people will talk about themselves and their work when they find themselves in a relaxed environment away from the workplace.

However, don't fall into the trap of becoming manipulative. Don't only try to see what's in it for you. Sometimes when you focus on others instead, you'll be astonished at the manner in which fairly unknown people will want to make contact and to work with you and your team.

There are strong similarities here with knowledge management (see page 26).

Goals and objectives are essential for individuals and groups. In teamwork, it's imperative for people to know where they are going. The ultimate destination is critical.

AIMING HIGH

'All the business of life is to endeavour.'

– Duke of Wellington

How to keep the goal in sight

We are all so busy at work that sometimes we cannot see the wood for the trees. It's vital to make sure that your team members are aware of the bigger picture. For people to know where they are going, they will need from you an overview of expectations. This will help them if they momentarily lose sight of the purpose of a task or the projected outcome of a project.

Even better, get the team involved in defining the future. In other words, don't wait to respond to change. Instead, create the sort of atmosphere in which your people can help establish the parameters for the way you work. Enable them to generate prospects and scenarios that they are committed to and so can help bring about.

Here is a model that could help you to sort out your strategy:

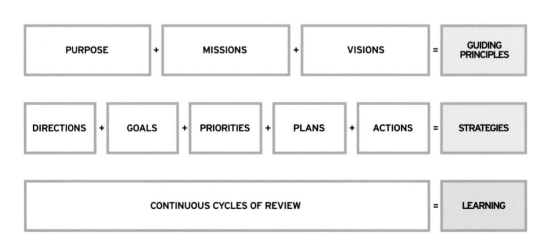

| PURPOSE | + | MISSIONS | + | VISIONS | = | GUIDING PRINCIPLES |

| DIRECTIONS | + | GOALS | + | PRIORITIES | + | PLANS | + | ACTIONS | = | STRATEGIES |

| CONTINUOUS CYCLES OF REVIEW | = | LEARNING |

DEFINING THE FUTURE

Here is a visual representation of the hierarchy
of elements needed to develop strategy:

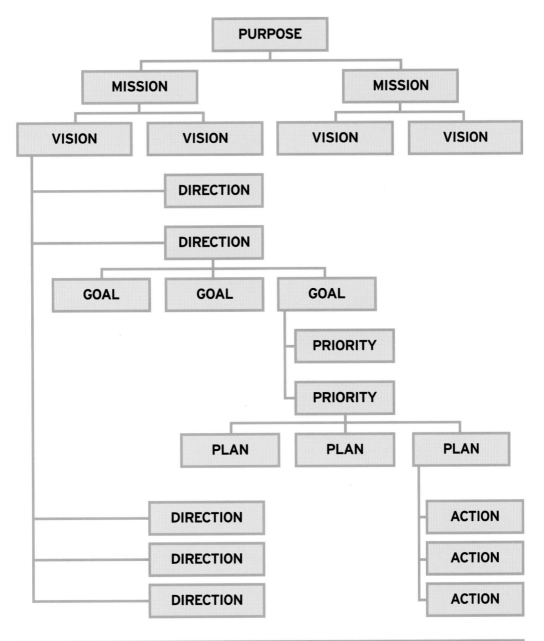

> '**Most of what we call management consists of making it difficult for people to get their work done.**'
>
> *– Peter Drucker*

The different elements of the strategic planning process can be outlined as follows:

1 Purpose
- Changes rarely
- Why do you do what you do?

2 Missions
- Key objective for the foreseeable future
- How will you implement your purpose?

3 Visions
- Long-term planning for the next five years
- What do you want to accomplish and by when?

4 Directions
- Five or six major themes
- Which activities will you focus upon?

5 Goals
- Short-term SMART targets (Specific, Measurable, Agreed, Realistic, Timely)
- Where are you aiming?

6 Priorities
- Allocating people, time, money, materials and facilities
- In what will you invest your (scarce) resources?

7 Plans
- Organizing, problem-solving and decision-making
- How will you actually achieve your expectations?

8 Actions
- Tangible, observable and measurable activities
- Which behaviours are most likely to fulfil the plan?

The entire strategic planning process must be based on continuous cycles of reflection, feedback and improvement. This will lead to learning at the organizational, departmental and individual levels.

Beware 'top-down' management

It is always dangerous to set or impose aims and objectives for others. Obviously, in many organizations this culture of top-down management exists, but the approach can lead to difficulties. It can create hostility or resentment, which may be unspoken. If the goals are unrealistic or inappropriate, then team members will feel cheated or betrayed. They may strive to accomplish them – and may even achieve them – but deep down they will not thank you for causing so much stress and anxiety. Similarly, if their aims and objectives are too easy, then team members will not value them. As a consequence, they may not value their work or role. Worse still, they could perhaps end up undervaluing you and the organization.

Of course, most of us can be lazy at times, and it is also tempting to always rely on the known and the comfortable. But this leads to complacency, and then to inaccuracy and mistakes. More importantly, it can mean that we disregard the needs of our stakeholders and customers. Eventually we will fail.

It is much better to involve your people in establishing their own goals, and to contribute to the process of setting targets for the team. This way, goals and targets are more likely to be achieved.

Performance management

Performance management is concerned with measuring and improving the work and output of an individual, a team and an organization – both quantitatively and qualitatively. According to researchers, there are two main ways of looking at performance management: the standards approach and the excellence appoach.

The standards approach
- Remedying poor performance
- Focuses on the individual
- Concentrates on underachievement
- Procedures – disciplinary, appraisal, incentives
- Transactional leadership

The excellence approach
- Enhancing strong performance
- Focuses on the team/organization
- Concentrates on continuous improvement
  - Conditions – coaching, motivation, commitment
    - Transformational leadership

The importance of balance
You need to keep all three elements (task, team and individual) in balance in performance management:

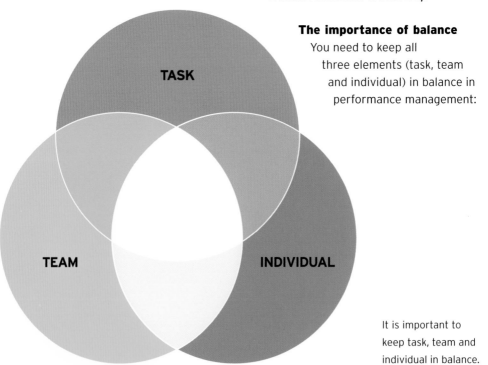

TASK

TEAM

INDIVIDUAL

It is important to keep task, team and individual in balance.

- Concern for the task – getting the job done
- Interest in the whole team – making sure that people are all pulling together in the same direction
- Attention to each individual – ensuring their differences are enhanced and their strengths used

Inevitably – and properly – there will be overlaps.

The criteria for performance management need to be agreed by all stakeholders. This must obviously include senior management, so that they can create the overall strategic plan. Additionally, functional managers will want to translate those larger goals into more manageable targets that relate to their own departments. And then your job as a team leader is to establish team and individual goals for your people.

Other stakeholders could include links in the supply chain, including customers, suppliers and even competitors and collaborators. Additionally, organizational goals need to be instituted in relation to shareholders or taxpayers, financial institutions or donors, and the media or advisers; and with regard to markets, resources and capacity.

For goals to have meaning, they must be relevant and up to date. Therefore, a five-year rolling plan needs to be revised just as frequently as the annual forecast. Such plans are not set in stone. They can – and must – be revised, reviewed and reworked in relation to both internal and external forces for change (see pages 93–99).

Increasingly, the criteria used in organizations to determine performance indicators are based on competencies. Such a framework can be simple and informal or complex and highly structured. The more sophisticated the scheme, the more beneficial the outcomes will be. Once competencies have been agreed as a result of wide consultation, they can be used for:

- **Recruitment schemes**
- **Reward strategies**
- **Development plans**
- **Outplacement activities**

Here is your chance to see what you think about teams, and how you fit in.

TEAMWORKING EXERCISES

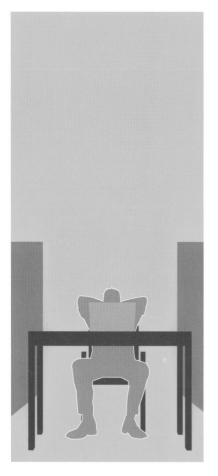

'I think we've been through a period where too many people have been given to understand that if they have a problem, it's the government's job to cope with it. "I have a problem, I'll get a grant." "I'm homeless, the government must house me." They're casting their problem on society. And, you know, there is no such thing as society. There are individual men and women, and there are families. And no government can do anything except through people, and people must look to themselves first. It's our duty to look after ourselves and then also to look after our neighbour. People have got the entitlements too much in mind, without the obligations. There's no such thing as entitlement, unless someone has first met an obligation.'

– Prime Minister Margaret Thatcher,
Women's Own magazine, 3 October 1987

'No man is an island, entire of itself; every man is a piece of the continent, a part of the main. If a clod be washed away by the sea, Europe is the less, as well as if a promontory were, as well as if a manor of thy friend's or of thine own were: any man's death diminishes me, because I am involved in mankind, and therefore never send to know for whom the bell tolls; it tolls for thee.'

– John Donne, 'Devotions upon Emergent Occasions, No. 17', 1624

Here are two different views of how people should relate together. Think about which one you agree with most and write down why.

Teamwork contributions quiz

This teamwork quiz will provide you with some important information on your preferred roles when working in a team.

Instructions

Read through the statements on pages 46–48. As you read, decide whether each one of them is very like you, fairly like you or not like you.

- If the statement is **very like you,** you score **2 points**
- If the statement is **fairly like you,** you score **1 point**
- If the statement is **not like you,** you score **0 points**

Your first response is likely to be the most accurate. Try to be honest and balanced in your responses. There are no right and wrong answers. Lie detectors have been built in! Don't try to second-guess the answers. Don't be too modest. As a help, focus on what you do more of and what you do less of. You are not trying to compare yourself with others, but rather this will help you identify your own strengths and weaknesses and those of the team.

Interpreting the results

Add up your scores using the chart on page 49. The questions are divided into eight statement groups, and you will have a score for each group.

Using the diagram on page 50, put a mark for the total scores for each of the statement groups on to the appropriate line – 0 is at the centre and 14 is at the end. Join up the marks to form a 'spider's web' of your own teamwork contributions profile.

Compare your 'spider's web' to the diagram on page 51, which reveals the dimensions of your profile. Read the descriptions on pages 52–56. Concentrate first of all on that role in which you had the **highest** score. Now do the same with your **lowest** score. How far do you agree with the comments? Why?

	STATEMENT	POINTS
1	I often produce original ideas.	
2	I pick up small mistakes that others fail to notice.	
3	I am a born organizer.	
4	I like to think more widely than the task in hand.	
5	My considered opinion is pretty close to the mark.	
6	I like to make my views count in the team.	
7	I like to finish everything I start.	
8	I can work with people who are very different.	
9	Working in a group cramps my imagination.	
10	I work best with people who have something to offer.	
11	I always maintain a wide range of contacts.	
12	My emotions seldom sway my judgement.	
13	I like to influence team decisions.	
14	Meeting targets is important to me.	
15	I pay attention to detail.	
16	I like to help team members with their problems.	
17	I can see the merits and failings of others' ideas.	
18	I often find new approaches to long-standing problems.	
19	I am good at co-ordinating various contributions.	

	STATEMENT	POINTS
20	I always see a job through to the end.	
21	I enjoy exploring new ideas.	
22	I like clearly defined goals when I am working.	
23	I like to get to know people well.	
24	I would risk unpopularity to get my views across.	
25	I have a creative approach to problems.	
26	I am a very practical person.	
27	I work hard to ensure agreement in the team.	
28	I can usually spot unsound ideas.	
29	I know who to contact if we need special information.	
30	I prefer to follow rather than to lead.	
31	I love work which requires a high level of concentration.	
32	I am always ready to emphasize my point of view.	
33	I get on well with others and work hard for the team.	
34	I usually take an independent view of problems.	
35	I keep up a steady pace whatever the pressure.	
36	I am assertive but respond to others' needs.	
37	I am happy to lead when action is needed.	
38	I like to know the latest ideas and developments.	

	STATEMENT	POINTS
39	I like time to weigh the options.	
40	I really enjoy being busy.	
41	I can relate ideas to new situations.	
42	I react strongly to time-wasting.	
43	I am good at reconciling differences.	
44	I will go along with most good suggestions.	
45	Urgency is part of my approach to work.	
46	I follow up interesting ideas and people.	
47	I am analytical in my approach to problems.	
48	I like to work step by step to a plan.	
49	I can sell an idea which I think is good.	
50	I am a conceptual thinker.	
51	I speak my mind.	
52	I can usually take a balanced view.	
53	I keep on the lookout for people who need help.	
54	Critical discernment appeals to me.	
55	I need my tasks clearly defined.	
56	I watch for difficulties.	

The questions on pages 46–48 are divided into eight different statement groups. Transfer your score for each question on to the chart below. For example, question number 1 is in group A, question number 2 is in group C, and so on. Once you have transfered all your scores, add up the total score for each statement group.

GROUP A	Statement	1	9	18	25	34	41	50		Total
	Points								=	
GROUP G	Statement	3	10	19	27	36	43	52		Total
	Points								=	
GROUP B	Statement	5	12	17	28	39	47	54		Total
	Points								=	
GROUP E	Statement	7	14	22	26	35	48	53		Total
	Points								=	
GROUP F	Statement	8	16	23	30	33	44	55		Total
	Points								=	
GROUP H	Statement	6	13	24	32	37	42	51		Total
	Points								=	
GROUP D	Statement	4	11	21	29	38	46	49		Total
	Points								=	
GROUP C	Statement	2	15	20	31	40	45	56		Total
	Points								=	

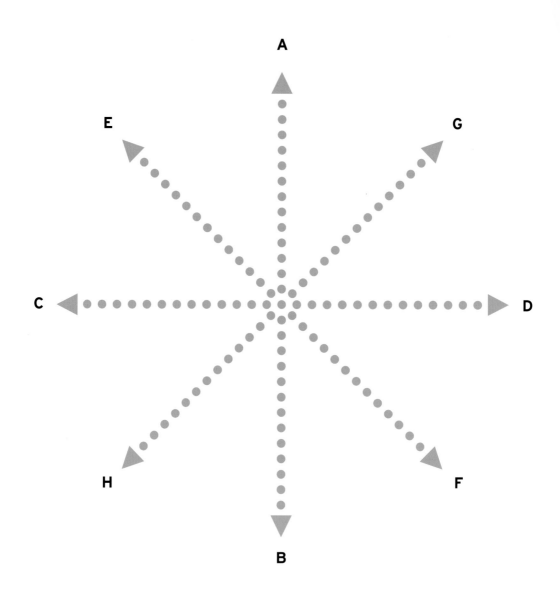

Put a mark for the total scores for each of the statement groups on to the appropriate line – 0 is at the centre and 14 is at the end. Join up the marks to form a 'spider's web' of your own profile. Compare your 'spider's web' to the diagram on page 51, which reveals the dimensions of your profile.

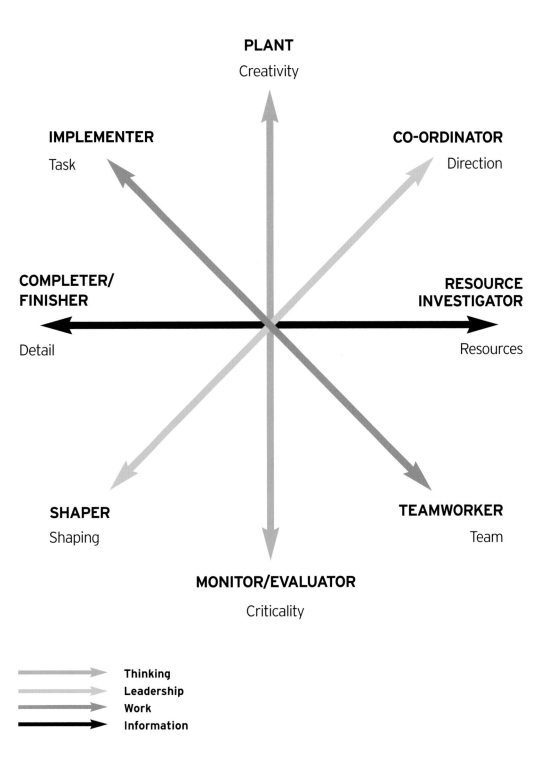

PLANT
Creativity

IMPLEMENTER
Task

CO-ORDINATOR
Direction

COMPLETER/
FINISHER

Detail

RESOURCE
INVESTIGATOR

Resources

SHAPER
Shaping

TEAMWORKER
Team

MONITOR/EVALUATOR
Criticality

Thinking
Leadership
Work
Information

TEAM ROLES

The personal skill inventory identifies eight team roles which are described below. Concentrate first of all on that role in which you had the **highest** score. Now do the same with your **lowest** score.

Shaper

Characteristics: Highly strung, outgoing, dynamic. Shapers are highly motivated people with a lot of nervous energy and a great need for achievement. Often they seem to be aggressive extroverts with strong drive. Shapers like to challenge, to lead and to push others into action – and to win. If obstacles arise, they will find a way round – but can be headstrong and emotional in response to any form of disappointment or frustration. Shapers can handle and even thrive on confrontation,

Function: Shapers generally make good managers because they generate action and thrive on pressure. They are excellent at sparking life into a team and are very useful in groups where political complications are apt to slow things down. Shapers are inclined to rise above problems of this kind and forge ahead regardless. They like making necessary changes and do not mind taking unpopular decisions. As the name implies, they try to impose some shape and pattern on group discussion or activities. They are probably the most effective members of a team in guaranteeing positive action.

Strengths: Drive and a readiness to challenge inertia, ineffectiveness, complacency or self-deception.

Allowable weaknesses: Prone to provocation, irritation and impatience, and a tendency to offend others.

Plant

Characteristics: Individualistic, serious-minded, unorthodox. Plants are innovators and inventors and can be highly creative. They provide the seeds and ideas from which major developments spring. Usually they prefer to operate by themselves at some distance from the other members of the team, using their imagination and often working in an unorthodox way. They tend to be introverted and react strongly to criticism and praise. Their ideas may often be radical and may lack practical constraint. They are independent, clever and original and may be weak in communicating with other people on a different wave-length.

Function: The main use of a Plant is to generate new proposals and to solve complex problems. Plants are often needed in the initial stages of a project or when a project is failing to progress. Plants have often made their marks as founders of companies or as originators of new products. Too many Plants in one organization, however, may be counter-productive as they tend to spend their time reinforcing their own ideas and engaging each other in combat.

Strengths: Genius, imagination, intellect, knowledge.

Allowable weaknesses: Up in the clouds, inclined to disregard practical details or protocol.

Co-ordinator *Chair*

Characteristics: Calm, self-confident, controlled. The distinguishing feature of Co-ordinators is their ability to cause others to work towards shared goals. Mature, trusting and confident, they delegate readily. In interpersonal relations they are quick to spot individual talents and to use them to pursue group objectives. While Co-ordinators are not necessarily the cleverest members of a team, they have a broad and worldly outlook and generally command respect.

Function: Co-ordinators are useful people to have in charge of a team with diverse skills and personal characteristics. They perform better in dealing with colleagues of near or equal rank than in directing junior subordinates. In some organizations, Co-ordinators are inclined to clash with Shapers due to their contrasting management styles.

Strengths: Welcome all potential contributors on their merits and without prejudice, but without ever losing sight of the main objective.

Allowable weaknesses: No pretensions as regards intellectual or creative ability.

Monitor-Evaluator

Characteristics: Sober, unemotional, prudent. Monitor-Evaluators are serious-minded, prudent individuals with a built-in immunity to being over-enthusiastic. They are slow deciders who prefer to think things over – usually with a high critical thinking ability. Good Monitor-Evaluators have a capacity for shrewd judgements that take all factors into account and seldom give bad advice.

Function: Monitor-Evaluators are at home when analysing problems and evaluating ideas and suggestions. They are very good at weighing up the pro's and con's of options and to outsiders seem dry, boring or even over-critical. Some people are surprised that they become managers. Nevertheless, many Monitor-Evaluators occupy key planning and strategic posts and thrive in high-level appointments where a relatively small number of decisions carry major consequences.

Strengths: Judgement, discretion, hard-headedness.

Allowable weaknesses: Lack of inspiration or the ability to motivate other people.

Resource Investigator

Characteristics: Extroverted, enthusiastic, curious, communicative. Resource Investigators are good communicators both inside and outside the organization. They are natural negotiators, adept at exploring new opportunities and developing contacts. Although not necessarily a great source of original ideas, they are quick to pick up other people's ideas and build on them. They are skilled at finding out what is available and what can be done, and usually get a warm welcome because of their outgoing nature. Resource Investigators have relaxed personalities with a strong inquisitive sense and a readiness to see the possibilities of anything new. However, unless they remain stimulated by others, their enthusiasm rapidly fades.

Function: Resource Investigators are quick to open up and exploit opportunities. They have an ability to think on their feet and to probe others for information. They are the best people to set up external contacts, to search for resources outside the group, and to carry out any negotiations that may be involved.

Strengths: A capacity for finding useful people and promising ideas or opportunities, and a general source of vitality.

Allowable weaknesses: Liable to lose interest after the initial fascination.

Implementer

Worker

Characteristics: Implementers are well organized, enjoy routine, and have a practical common-sense and self-discipline. They favour hard work and tackle problems in a systematic fashion. On a wider front they hold unswerving loyalty to the organization and are less concerned with the pursuit of self-interest. However, Implementers may find difficulty in coping with new situations.

Function: Implementers are useful because of their reliability and capacity for application. They succeed because they have a sense of what is feasible and relevant. It is said that many executives only do the jobs they wish to do and neglect those tasks that they find distasteful. By contrast, Implementers will do what needs to be done. Good Implementers often progress to high management positions by virtue of good organizational skills and efficiency in dealing with all necessary work.

Strengths: Organizing ability, practical common sense, hard working, self-discipline.

Allowable weaknesses: Lack of flexibility, resistance to unproven ideas.

Completer-Finisher

Characteristics: Painstaking, orderly, conscientious, anxious. Completers, or Completer-Finishers, have a great capacity for follow-through and attention to detail, and seldom start what they cannot finish. They are motivated by internal anxiety, although outwardly they may appear unruffled. Typically, they are introverts who don't need much external stimulus or incentive. Completer-Finishers dislike carelessness and are intolerant of those with a casual disposition. Reluctant to delegate, they prefer to tackle all tasks themselves.

Function: Completer-Finishers are invaluable where tasks demand close concentration and a high degree of accuracy. They foster a sense of urgency within a team and are good at meeting schedules. In management, they excel by the high standards to which they aspire, and by their concern for precision, attention to detail and follow-through.

Strengths: A capacity for fulfilling their promises and working to the highest standards.

Allowable weaknesses: A tendency to worry about small things and a reluctance to 'let go'.

Team Worker

Characteristics: Socially oriented, rather mild and sensitive. Team Workers are the most supportive members of a team. They are mild, sociable and concerned about others with a great capacity for flexibility and adapting to different situations and people. Team Workers are perceptive and diplomatic. They are good listeners and are generally popular members of a group. They cope less well with pressure or situations involving the need for confrontation.

Function: A Team Worker's role is to prevent interpersonal problems within a team and allow everyone to contribute effectively. Since they don't like friction, they will go to great lengths to avoid it. The diplomatic and perceptive skills of a Team Worker become real assets, especially under a managerial regime where conflicts are liable to arise or to be artificially suppressed. Team Worker managers are not seen as a threat and therefore can be elected as the most accepted and favoured people to serve under. People seem to co-operate better when they are around.

Strengths: Ability to respond to people and situations and to promote team spirit.

Allowable weaknesses: Indecision at moments of crisis and some failure to provide a clear lead to others.

A balanced team

The ideal team will have all these roles represented equally, and by those with very high scores! On your own, you can never achieve this, but with your other team members ... well, anything is possible!

Remember, your weaknesses are likely to be matched by other people's strengths – and *vice versa*! Another important thing to remember is that you also have a second and a third strength as well. So, if in your team there are several of you good at, say, 'shaping', then you should decide to concentrate instead on showing more of your other strong roles, such as being a 'plant' or a 'co-ordinator' if the team lacks these roles in other people. A colloquial English phrase for this is *having a second string to your bow*!

Now have a look at this picture. Where do you see yourself fitting in? Which person do you identify with most? Why is that? How would you go about improving yourself in that position? Do you want to be different? How will you go about such change?

Summary

- Your team is far greater than the sum of its parts
- Your team needs to be effective as well as efficient
- Your team must work more closely together
- Your team comprises a rich spectrum of diverse individuals
- Your team should determine its key results areas
- Your team will thrive on feedback
- Your team has to know where it's going if it's going to get there
- Your team must keep an eye on what's happening elsewhere
- Your team requires constant care and attention
- Your team has a wealth of knowledge that needs tapping into

2 LEADING YOUR TEAM

Over the years people have argued long and hard about whether leaders are born or made, whether leadership is something you just have or something you can learn.

WHAT MAKES A GOOD TEAM LEADER?

For some, those who seem heroic in everything they do, managing to win against all the odds, are obviously born leaders. But others insist that there is no genetic component to leadership at all, just qualities such as vision and direction that can be learned in a variety of ways. The divide can be characterized as an exclusive versus an inclusive approach.

Despite decades of research, the jury is still out because the experts just can't agree about the origins and development of leadership qualities. However, based on many studies in different types of organization in a variety of settings, there is general consensus on what those qualities actually are. Each of the sections that follow will be devoted to one aspect of good leadership, so read on!

There is one thing that needs to be made absolutely clear from the beginning: leadership is about action, not position!

'A quality which is prominent in every leader is a strongly developed sense of dominant purpose and direction in life. He is one who knows with greater than average strength of conviction what he wants to get done, and where he wants to go. '

– Ordway Tead

Leadership qualities

Most people agree that a good leader has most of these qualities:

- Vision
- Respect
- Rapport
- Sense of humour
- Inspiration
- Dedication
- Open mindedness

Involving your team

The best leaders will always involve the people in their teams by:

- Communicating
- Consulting
- Delegating
- Empowering
- Listening
- Asking
- Developing

HEALTH WARNING!

Don't panic. Don't disqualify yourself yet as we haven't even begun. Don't think you can't do it just because you're daunted by the very prospect of leading a team. And forget about anyone who has ever told you that you'll never make a good leader.

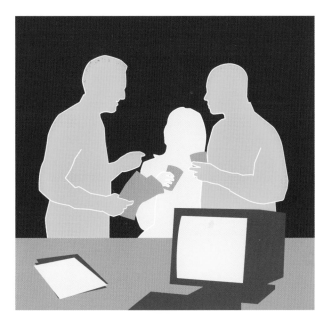

'A good objective of leadership is to help those who are doing poorly to do well, and to help those who are doing well to do even better.'

– Jim Rohn

Most people start new jobs because of pay, promotion or power, but most leave because they can't stand the working conditions or their manager any more.

EMPOWERING YOUR TEAM

When asked in exit interviews why they are leaving, many employees say, 'He is a bully' or 'She just won't let me get on with things' or 'The bosses around here are too bossy!'

You need to let people do their jobs

Most of us don't like being watched when we're at work. Basically, we imagine that the manager doesn't trust us, won't treat us like an adult and is checking up on us. In some places, the approach is to breathe down people's necks until they do as they're told. For example, if you are only five minutes late for work, you'd think that the sky had fallen down!

One problem is that many of us have learned to do our jobs differently from the way we were trained in the first place, often with considerable improvements. But being watched makes us revert to the 'proper' way, conforming to expected patterns of working. Such conformity tends to stifle creativity and initiative. So, instead of always checking to see if your team has done what they've been told to do, why not allow them space and time to get on with their jobs?

Don't be tempted to think you have to muscle in on what they're doing all the time. Give them room to do it their own way. Give them the opportunity to prioritize tasks by themselves. Give them a chance to come up with their own answers to a problem first. And then, only if you find that they're having difficulties or making mistakes, you can ask them how they have been organizing their work.

Don't imagine that you have to be an expert in every aspect of your team's job either. Even in massive organizations where new entrants traditionally start at the lowest level, because top managers feel that they should understand that job first before being promoted, there are eventually opportunities to specialize and develop. So no senior executive is ever going to know everything about every job being done by every member of staff in the hierarchy beneath them.

THE THREE COMMANDMENTS

1 **Give people space to work on their own**

2 **Give people time to think things through for themselves**

3 **Trust people to do it their way**

Take your hands off the controls and trust your team!

When you do start to trust your team and can stand back a bit, you will have more opportunities to observe what people do, rather than simply relying on their assessments of what they do. The two can be quite different!

If workers are treated as children, with their manager acting as a stern headmaster, they will often behave accordingly and conflict will ensue. However, most people flourish if they are trusted and respected as mature adults.

Writers trying to explain the intricacies of human motivation have spilt gallons of ink over the years.

BOOSTING YOUR TEAM

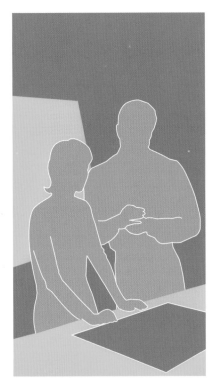

Some pet theories have come and gone, while others have remained unquestioned for decades. Suffice to say, there is no easy way to understand why someone decides to do something. The individuals themselves might not even be fully aware of what really makes them tick.

You need to encourage people to perform

The verb 'to encourage' means literally 'to put heart into someone'. Basically, you need to build your people up, overcome their doubts and help them deal with their anxieties.

As a leader, one of your primary responsibilities is to make sure your team does more than merely turn up for work. We are not talking about you suddenly becoming a slave-driver – far from it! But if team members are to work more effectively and more efficiently, then they will need you to help them.

And it's how you help that matters, because you cannot treat everyone the same. It's not just a case of different people liking different things. It's more to do with finding out what makes each person put in that little bit extra effort.

How to go about it

You need to get to know people as individuals. Of course, there will be times when you have to meet together as a team, but you must also invest quality time with each and every member of your team on their own. Just by spending a short while with each person, giving them your undivided attention and focusing on their issues, you will show that you value them for themselves and not just as one of a number of workers in the department, office or shop.

While you're all there to do a job, and it's important to talk about work-related issues, don't restrict your conversation to issues such as whether or not they're meeting their targets or achieving their performance indicators.

Since it's going to take time to get to know your team, aim to meet with each person for short, regular periods – say, ten minutes once a week. Don't try to save these meetings up for an hour every couple of months. That can be daunting for even the most accomplished professional in your team, and you would find it a strain too.

You also need to sponsor risk-taking in your team, so encourage people to try things out, to take the initiative and to experiment with change – all in a positive atmosphere. If they are constantly looking over their shoulders, waiting for you to come down on them like a ton of bricks every time they make a mistake, they won't even try. However, in the absence of fear and recrimination, once there is genuine and sincere support you will see remarkable developments among your team.

'Outstanding leaders go out of their way to boost the self-esteem of their personnel. If people believe in themsleves, it's amazing what they can accomplish.'

– *Sam Walton*

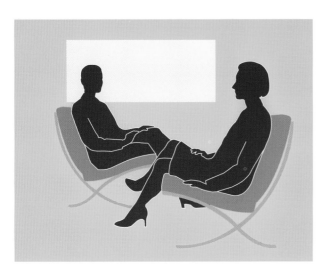

However much experience members of your team already have, there is always going to be room for more training. And once you start asking people to undertake new tasks, they will learn.

FACILITATING LEARNING

You must remain focused at all times on those who are learning.

You need to foster a learning environment

Instruction for people at work usually takes two forms: coaching and mentoring. In academic circles, the battle still rages about the differences between these two forms of on-the-job training. Definitions abound, but these usually reveal more about the writers' personal preferences and prejudices than anything else.

For our purposes, coaching and mentoring both have useful roles to play. In certain areas, their contributions might overlap, but in others they offer distinctive approaches to the learning process.

There are both similarities and differences between mentoring and coaching. For our purposes here, it is important to concentrate on what they have in common, namely the skills and techniques you will use to help your team members to develop.

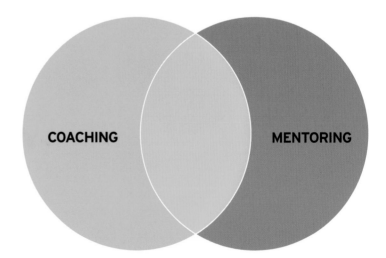

COACHING · MENTORING

Coaching and mentoring are different, but both methods share similar skills and techniques.

Coaching is a method of helping employees to develop their knowledge, skills and attitudes in relation to a new job or task. Mentoring is a means of enabling them to take responsibility for the wider aspects of their job and career. The area of overlap is to be found in the techniques that are used. Both approaches will need considerable patience on your part. You must remain focused at all times on those who are learning. You are not there to teach them so much as to help them to learn. You must be organized, thorough and methodical in your ways of working. It is also essential that you develop a good, open, trusting relationship.

Coaching

There are two aspects to helping someone learn a new skill. First, you need to take a long, hard look at the bigger picture. This means:

Identifying the gap
In other words, what are the person's goals and needs? How can you support them? Here you are gathering information about the person: where they are, where they want to be and the perceived challenges they face.

Collecting valid information
Observe their behaviour and gather information. Observation is a crucial part of the process, since you will need to be as specific and accurate as possible.

Identifying the areas to work on
Decide what information, when shared with the person, will have the greatest impact on their performance.

Sharing feedback and ideas
Give the person feedback on what you've observed and make suggestions for improvement, setting action plans for follow-up steps where appropriate.

Keep moving forward
Hold together the person's new skills and behaviours. As a coach you can assist the person to find opportunities to practise and build on these skills.

Secondly, you need to focus on the practical aspects of helping someone to carry out a new task. Here is a step-by-step approach to coaching or job instruction:

Step 1 Prepare all the materials, tools and equipment
Plan the learning environment.

Step 2 Gain the person's attention
Introduce the purpose and context of the task; explain Health and Safety aspects; show the tools, materials and equipment to be used.

Step 3 Demonstrate the whole task at a normal pace
Discuss important points of the task; get the person to describe what they have seen and heard; ask open questions to determine understanding.

Step 4 Model the first part of the task slowly
Repeat and encourage the person to imitate you at the same time; assist them in practising this first part to achieve standards; repeat the process for the second part; link the two parts.

Step 5 Continue until the whole task is complete
Test the achievement of learning objectives; facilitate feedback to improve long-term memory; give opportunity to practise.

Step 6 Evaluate short- and medium-term changes to job behaviour and performance improvement

Mentoring

It is not a good idea to mentor people in your own team, as the blurring of roles is very difficult to manage – for you both. However, you could easily swap mentoring responsibilities with another team leader.

At your first meeting, you will need to establish the ground rules and work out how you intend to proceed.

- Concentrate initially on getting to know each other and building rapport
- Agree how you will work together: contact points/message protocol/cancellation of meetings; frequency/length/venue of meetings; confidentiality/contact outside meetings; agreed boundaries – for example, does the relationship cover personal as well as work issues?
- Draw up a mentoring agreement: ascertain whether any additional ground rules are required; sign the agreement and both keep copies
- Establish what each of you wants to get out of the scheme: prepare for this before the meeting; discuss your goals and how you might go about achieving them; ascertain the current situation of the person you are mentoring; they should describe this and what their role involves
- Have an initial discussion of the career ambitions of the person you are mentoring
- List action points and deadlines arising from the first meeting
- Agree date and venue of next meeting

HOW TO BE A SUCCESSFUL MENTOR

- Believe in the mentoring process
- Accept the person you are mentoring unconditionally
- Provide learning support in different contexts
- Model continuous learning
- Provide hope and optimism
- Be an active listener
- See and explain the bigger picture
- Be analytical, critical and evaluative
- Have advanced business and interpersonal skills

'The final test of a leader is that he leaves behind him in other people the conviction to carry on.'

– Walter Lippman

IDEAS FOR FUTURE MENTORING SESSIONS

- Help the person you are mentoring to undertake a SWOT analysis (SWOT stands for Strengths, Weaknesses, Opportunities and Threats), then create action points on outcomes

- Give them a practice interview

- Discuss any problems that they are experiencing at work and help them to work through these

- Discuss any training that they have undertaken in the past year and its usefulness

- Discuss any continuous professional development (CPD) activities they have undertaken in the past year. (CPD includes a whole range of different activities in addition to training courses, such as formal education programmes; conferences and seminars; secondments and attachments; reading, reflecting and thinking; and visits and shadowing.) Ask them to bring a record of a CPD activity undertaken to each meeting. This should include answers to the following: what did you do, why did you do it, what did you learn from this, how have you used this (or how will you use this) and are you planning any further action?

- Discuss what they could do to improve the work of their department/organization and help them to formulate their ideas and implementation processes

- Discuss their visibility within their organization and how they can raise their profile

- Have a session planning their career ambitions for various points in the future. Look at what skills they have but lack for the next stage, then go on to consider and discuss how they might acquire them

- Consider their understanding of wider management issues and whether they should be working on this

- Look at their CV (ask them to produce one if it doesn't already exist) and suggest ways in which it might be improved

- Spot tomorrow's issues in their field of work, thus helping them to stay ahead and be ready for the future

- Discuss the importance of networking and help them to improve their skills in this area

- Discuss their last performance appraisal

MENTORING SESSION RECORD

Date:

1 Status of items on which I've worked since the last meeting

2 Goals for today

3 Current issues

4 Options based upon current issues

5 Proposed actions (what, by when, resources needed)

6 Things to think about or work to do in the future

Above is an example of a mentoring session record you could use.

Encouraging progress

Having started to help your team by arranging coaching and mentoring, it's just as important not to stop there. It's your responsibility to promote a sense of lifelong learning among your team. Organizations need to embrace and manage change constantly if they are to survive. Departments must adapt and adjust to the organization's new strategies and policies, while employees will want to stay ahead in the fiercely competitive job market. So you need to help them to learn how to learn.

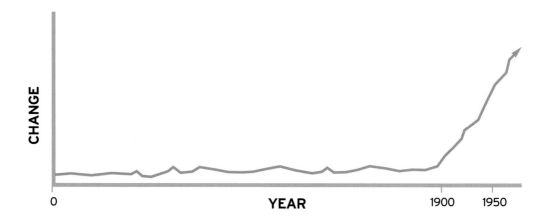

CHANGE

0   **YEAR**   1900   1950

This graph shows that over time the rate of change has accelerated.

The diagram above shows that there has always been a certain amount of change, but in the last 50 years or so there has been more change than in the rest of the history of civilization put together. For example, in about 1900, the invention of the car dramatically changed how people worked, where they lived, and how they enjoyed their leisure. Similarly, with the introduction and development of the computer since 1950, our lives have been altered beyond recognition! And of course there have been many other inventions, developments and discoveries in the realms of medicine, education, housing, and transportation.

Change is here to stay! The only thing we know for sure is that things will change. What the diagram shows is that there has been more change in your lifetime than in the last 2,000 years. And the rate of change is accelerating.

To give you an example, when my grandmother was born there were no such things as aeroplanes. Now, however, we are quite used to travelling in them, to any part of the globe, in less than a day. And to while away the time, we can easily use the in-seat facilities – phone, videos, CDs and computer games – before writing our next book on the laptop!

No longer can we merely wait for change to happen and then try to respond. Instead, it is vitally important to anticipate change, to plan for it and then to make it happen. The way forward is to develop at all levels – organizational, team and individual.

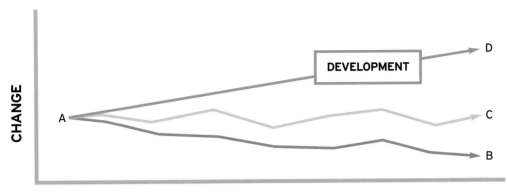

In the diagram above, at starting point **A**, there are three choices we could make.

First, we could decide to do nothing. We're quite happy where we are and comfortable in our accomplishments. We don't see any need to change the way we've always done things. Now, if that is our attitude – or our organization's policy – then we will end up at **B**. In other words, we will not continue to exist. There is no sustainable future in this approach. Even government departments are not immune to the gravitational pull of self-satisfied complacency.

Second, we could decide to respond and react to every change as it comes along. We'll just wait and see what happens. We won't rock the boat too much. We're just interested in looking after ourselves and our jobs. In that case, we will end up at **C**. We'll do the bare minimum to reduce the amount of change necessary and keep our heads above water. The problem is – the water's rising! Ultimately, we will be overtaken by others.

Third, we could decide to be proactive, to make the change happen. We could analyse our current situation and determine where we want to be at some point in the future. This way, we would end up at **D**. Then we could formulate a strategy to make it happen.

Development is all about extending the competency, capability and capacity of your team – that is, the people in it. As a leader, you must challenge complacency and lazy assumptions.

This graph illustrates three different attitudes to change. You can do nothing (B), you can respond and react to change (C) or you can be proactive and make change happen (D).

Empowerment in business means giving power to others. Power can come with your position, your age or your experience. It can reside in the size of your budget or the grandeur of your office.

GIVING IT ALL AWAY

You need to practise 'servant leadership'

Too often, power conjures up pictures of one person imposing their will on another. Bullying has no place in modern leadership. While such behaviour might gain a short-term advantage, in the long run relationships will at best be soured and at worst damaged beyond repair, with employees resigning. By insisting on getting their own way, bad managers like these might well claim to be focusing on the needs of the organization, but only at the expense of their workers. And even those workers who seem to be acceding to their requirements in public will distance themselves from such policies or practices in private. They will seek ways to get promoted, transferred or made redundant. If all else fails, they may even try to get the manager discredited or, worse still, become subversive.

Power in organizations these days can be gained in a most paradoxical manner. You get more by giving it away! This is what is known as servant leadership and one of its hallmarks is empowerment.

As the leader, you will be asked to make charitable donations – that is, free gifts to others, expecting nothing in return! Obviously, you are not going to be giving money, although what you do give will be just as valuable. There are four major areas where you need to make constant provision for the people in your team.

Trust

When your team members receive your trust, they will accept the faith you put in them. Once they feel that they are valuable, so their sense of self-worth will develop. Since they know you are giving them responsibility, they will become responsible. From this, they will take pride in their work, develop loyalty for the team and show willingness to follow your lead.

Time

Time is a most valuable commodity and so you need to spend it liberally on your team. As you invest quality time with them – both together and individually – you will reap dividends. You don't have to spend ages with them, although formal one-to-one sessions are important on a regular basis. Here we're talking about devoting precious moments to offer advice, motivation and kindness. They will feel noticed and needed, sensing that their opinions have been heard and appreciated. Even if you don't always agree with them, they will be aware of your underlying principles of justice and equity.

Tools

Too often we don't allow our employees to perform effectively because we hamper them through a lack of basic resources. As a leader, you must make sure that they have the right materials, equipment and space necessary to do a good job. They will expect you to fight for scarce resources on their behalf. A shortage of basic supplies or facilities will do more to undermine their efforts than inadequate procedures or systems. This may mean being a pioneer as you insist on your team having the best or latest equipment. It could result in your becoming unpopular with other leaders as you ensure that your team has a fair slice of the cake.

Training

Effective leaders must ensure that their team has the knowledge, skills and attitudes necessary to perform their work to a good standard. Courses, seminars, conferences and workshops are all important. But so too are regular coaching, mentoring and job instruction. You're not expected to be an ace performer, but you should at the very least make sure you take the time to learn presentation skills and attend a 'train-the-trainer' programme.

WARNING

Beware activities that are little more than an excuse for running round in a field, jumping over barrels and tying planks together with pieces of rope!

Concrete is a very good building material, but it becomes stronger once it is reinforced with steel rods. It's the same with your team.

STRENGTHENING AND SUPPORTING YOUR TEAM

'No problem is insurmountable. With a little courage, teamwork and determination, a person can overcome anything.'

– B. Dodge

If you are going to build a strong group of people who will work together to achieve individual and group targets, then you need to provide the human equivalent of those steel rods.

You need to find ways to reinforce the team

There are five interlocking disciplines that will provide you with the necessary tools:

• Systems thinking
• Personal mastery
• Mental models
• Shared vision
• Team learning

Systems thinking
Expansionist thinking

Since standing still and doing nothing is no longer an option, you need to support your team by pushing the boundaries of their expectations – and yours too. Think big! Ask questions like, 'Why not?' and 'What's stopping us?'

A number of consultants have advised their clients to 'think outside the box'. Essentially, leaders must critically examine all assumptions and set patterns of working. Don't feel afraid to ask what might appear to be naïve questions.

You also need to be on the lookout for new directions and opportunities. 'Where next?' is a question that should come easily to you. Be prepared to find the answer in unexpected places, outside of your immediate working group, department, organization or profession. Mix with people unlike you. Read widely. Anticipate change before it happens.

Connective understanding

Make links and draw things together. Enable people to associate in new and unusual working relationships, both within the team and outside it. Play to their strengths. Look more widely than the here-and-now in order to produce exciting new possibilities. Familiarize yourself with people's abilities as well as their needs. In this way you will be able to stretch them by putting them in touch with others who can develop them in ways you can't.

Intuition

Sometimes you will make decisions that are not based on analysis, intellect or logic. You will find that – with experience, common sense and your understanding of the organization and its people – you are able to make assessments and reach conclusions that at first sight might appear strange or unusual. Good leaders recognize that they often 'fly by the seat of their pants', 'go with their gut reaction' and 'trust their intuition'.

Your team members will learn to trust such decisions, particularly when they take account of the human aspects, rather than just relying on a dry and rational examination of charts, figures and accounts.

Perspective integration

Look for the big picture. Deliberately hunt out new vistas. Try to see things from other people's point of view. Then include these brand-new ideas into your existing policies, practices, procedures and plans.

When walking in the countryside, one of the best ways to avoid getting lost is occasionally to look behind you and view the landscape from a different perspective – what does it look like coming from the opposite direction? It's exactly the same where you work. Ask yourself how this project or that deadline will seem to the people from Marketing or Supplies. How will the finance director see your new proposition?

Personal mastery

On my bookshelves at home, there are probably 70 or more books on Leadership or Teamwork, but there is not a single volume entitled 'Followership'! And yet leaders need followers! You could say that unless a leader has got people willing to follow them, then they will have nobody to lead. So what makes a good follower, or team member? The two lists below show how leadership competencies are matched by followership expectations:

LEADERSHIP COMPETENCIES	FOLLOWERSHIP EXPECTATIONS
Compassion	Encouragement
Self-acceptance	Acceptance
Acceptance of others	Empowerment
Ability to share power	Trust
Authenticity	Self-discovery
Nurturing of spirit	Someone worth working for
Moral leadership	Dignity
Sensitivity	Autonomy
Humility	Fulfilled potential
Mastery	Growth
Growth-oriented	Supported choice
Risk-taker	Independence
Self-directed	Space to make mistakes
Tolerant of ambiguity	Support in transition
Value-based	Learning
Trusting	Responsibility
Spiritual	Self/other connection
Self-subordinating	Ownership of results

Mental models
Insight
Occasionally you will find that you are able to make unexpected leaps in your understanding of a situation. The facts as presented may lead to a dead-end in your thinking until, suddenly, you find a new and dynamic relationship between previously unrelated details. Such a jump is sometimes referred to as insight and usually requires a considerable amount of background knowledge of the situation and its context.

Creative perceptions of this sort are often based upon experience, but can also be found in those with great mental agility or lively imaginations. The important thing is to keep suggesting alternatives, choices and ranges, without being constrained by the normal or the predictable. In this way you will 'discover' solutions in amazing and wonderful ways.

Challenge assumptions
There is not a single policy, procedure, practice or plan in any organization that cannot be improved in some way. Just because workers have been doing something in a certain way for years doesn't mean that it always has to be done like that. Those very methods of working were originally introduced to change how things had been done previously.

Focus on priorities
Let's assume that you have four jobs to do. How will you decide which to tackle first? One of them is considered very urgent and very important (1), while another is considered neither urgent nor important (4). You can plot them on a chart like the one below.

MORE URGENT		1 ✓
LESS URGENT	4 ✗	
	LESS IMPORTANT	**MORE IMPORTANT**

The problem comes when trying to decide where to put tasks 2 and 3.

Some people tend to always tackle the urgent jobs first, while others prefer to concentrate on the important ones. In deciding on the best approach, you need to consider the consequences – not of doing something, but of *not* doing it! Who has asked for the job to be done? Who will be affected by any delay? Are there savings to be made or will costs be incurred if you do the job now as opposed to later? And more importantly, can the job be delegated to someone else?

Obviously, the best way to determine priorities is to see them as part of the overall strategic plans that have been developed for the organization, department and team. This will avoid the need to respond in a purely reactive way once a potentially damaging situation has already arisen.

Innovation

Consider this diagram (left). It shows how, in organizations, products and services are always being developed to meet newly identified needs. There are also numerous tangible and not so tangible items that are considered valuable to the smooth running of operations. But it's only when the new and the valuable overlap that you can have true innovation.

If something is both new and valuable, then there will be innovation. The patent registries of the world are full of amazing new inventions that are absolutely worthless! Consequently, they have never been manufactured or produced for a mass market. One example was a self-inflating car tyre. Alternatively, much that is taken as being of value to people and organizations is not new. Too often, there is a mere re-cycling of the old, familiar, comfortable developments from the past, such as the client database system that creaks and groans under the weight of having to produce reports in a way that was never intended when it was first introduced. So there cannot be innovation. A good example of innovation was the introduction of the clockwork radio, where the problem of finding a new energy source was solved by creatively employing one

Innovation occurs when something is both new and valuable.

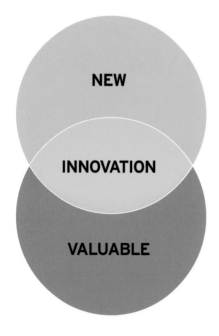

technology (a wind-up mechanism and spring) in a new context (broadcasting) with the result that radios can now be used by people in situations where the availability of batteries or electricity is scarce.

Shared vision

Sometimes called 'the psychological contract', this is a way of looking at the unspoken relationship that exists between an employer and the workforce. It can be seen as a two-way exchange between the parties.

The two lists opposite illustrate an aspect of this 'psychological contract' of people at work. There is a giving and receiving by both parties. In a really effective team or organization there will be many similarities between the two. In some places this is known as 'alignment'.

Team learning

Most of the learning that takes place where you work will be the result of work carried out by individuals. However, there will also be occasions when the whole team can learn together – with and from each other, as well as with the help of others.

You will probably find that as you facilitate learning by modelling patterns of good practice, so team members will grow more confident about using them too. This in turn will help the whole team to demonstrate these competencies:

- Encourage relationships
- Co-operation
- Dialogue
- Listening
- Creativity
- Promote harmony

Taking the whole team on a team-building exercise away from the workplace is potentially advantageous. If you select a skilled facilitator who can help you to transfer the learning back into the working environment, then the team will benefit from the closer bonds formed through trust and direction.

GIVE AND TAKE

If you offer:
- Principles
- Alignment of organizational and personal values
- Inspiration
- Goals
- Vision
- Vitality
- Motivation
- Commitment

Your team will have:
- Sense of purpose
- Alignment of personal and organizational values
- Motivation
- Clarity
- Shared vision
- Engagement
- Commitment

Employees are constantly having to work harder and for longer. Recessions and redundancies have resulted in downsizing, re-engineering and outsourcing.

LOOKING BEYOND THE IMMEDIATE

'A man to carry on a successful business must have imagination. He must see things as in a vision, a whole dream of the whole thing.'

– Charles Schwab

Many workers sometimes feel they are expendable and superfluous. And rising income levels don't necessarily create any greater degree of tenure or security. Whether you are a famous football player, a pop star, a fashion icon or a managing director, you can still be sold – or sold out – on the whim of your boss.

You need to aim for sustainability

Away from work, many people find themselves caught up in a frenzy of panic-buying or engaging in 'retail therapy'. As a result, greater demands are being put upon suppliers to provide more for less.

With increased consumerism in Western society came a constant need – or so we were led to believe – for customers' requirements to be met immediately. Standardized products and services had to be offered to a consistently high standard in a range of locations, or an ever-changing array of new merchandise had be presented in an effort to catch customers' attention and affect their buying decisions. This has been linked to the increasing trend towards globalization, where the 'one size fits all' approach ignores centuries of cultural difference and ethnic diversity. It is what has been disparagingly termed 'McDonaldization'.

The marketing backlash

However, at the very time when most high streets and shopping malls had become predictably similar, there was a growth in small, specific, unusual outlets catering for niche markets. Customers were suddenly on the lookout for something different.

In such a complex, fluctuating and differentiated marketplace, purchasers sometimes desire a more predictable, secure and unsurprising supply chain. This has led to the greatest need of most organizations: to achieve greater sustainability.

And so it is with our teams as well. We must resist a constant striving for the newest, the latest or the most fashionable business techniques or management trends. Instead, it is our responsibility to ensure a future for our people – and therefore our organizations.

To use athletics as a metaphor, we must help individuals to see their work not so much in terms of a 100-metre sprint but more as a ten-kilometre jog. Better still, the team should see it as a group fun-run, where their position will depend on both individual performances and joint accomplishment.

For this they will require a different training schedule, a new outlook and a changed mentality. Techniques, tactics and planning will all be altered. Moreover, greater value will have to be placed on determination, perseverance and strength of character. The ability to overcome obstacles rather than giving up or running away must be central to your team's success.

Here are some important elements you will need if you and your team are to achieve sustainable growth:

- Preparing
- Planning
- Purchasing
- Providing
- Partying

Preparing – good practice

It has been argued that much of the training that is carried out these days is short term in its approach and historical in its orientation. Many people at work are sent on the wrong courses, at the wrong times and for the wrong reasons. On the other hand, military units spend most of their time training, getting ready for the very occasional battle. Therefore, we must have a good training policy for the team and effective learning plans for those in it.

TRAINING POLICY

There are certain vital elements that must be included in any training policy.

- Commitment from senior management/board
- Responding to the needs of the organization
- Named senior manager responsible for implementation
- Roles of all those contributing to training
- Responsibilities of individual employees
- Acceptable and realistic resources
- Learning strategies
- Diversity and access
- Funding/budgets
- Process for identifying/analysing training needs
- Performance management/measurement
- Individual/Career/Succession/Organization/Management development plans
- Systematic training and development
- External quality standards

What level of consultation will there be?

How will the policy be communicated?

How will it be implemented?

How will it be reviewed?

THE LEARNING PLAN

Learner's Name:

Team leader:

Department:

Trainer/Mentor/Coach:

1 Which specific learning need has been identified?

2 What other learning needs does this relate to, either for yourself or for others you work with?

3 What is your learning objective?

4 What is your preferred learning style?

5 By when would you like the learning to be completed?

6 What constraints can you identify that could limit the effectiveness of your learning?

7 What will you do after the training in order to implement your learning and so improve your work?

Signed:

Employee: **Date:**

Manager: **Date:**

Trainer: **Date:**

This is the classic approach to systematic training (right). But in order to move from a circle to a cycle, you must use the evaluation to analyse future needs (below).

TRAINING NEEDS ANALYSIS

EVALUATING TRAINING

PLANNING AND DESIGNING TRAINING

DELIVERING TRAINING

TRAINING NEEDS ANALYSIS

EVALUATING TRAINING

PLANNING AND DESIGNING TRAINING

DELIVERING TRAINING

TRAINING NEEDS ANALYSIS

EVALUATING TRAINING

PLANNING AND DESIGNING TRAINING

DELIVERING TRAINING

It is good practice is to adopt a systematic approach to training and development (see the top diagram). Even better, we should implement this not as a circle but as an ongoing cycle.

Planning – good direction

Well in advance of the event, marathon runners are given a detailed map of the route. The organizers will also paint a line on the road for them to follow and, in addition, there will be a car or motorbike for the leaders to chase. This means that the runners will all be covering the same ground, in the same direction.

In a similar way, you should provide a route map for your team. This will serve to keep them together and make sure they are all going the same way. In other words, they will all see the same vision.

However, don't think that you have to create the map on your own. Senior management and departmental executives will inevitably have their own ideas and strategic plans, and yours will need to fit into these and help to implement them.

Moreover, your people must be given opportunities to contribute to the plan. That way, having been part of the process, they will feel that their contribution is valued and worthwhile. They will want to see the goal accomplished and will be motivated to work hard over a much longer period. And knowing which way to go – which route to follow – will relieve them of much of the stress that comes from working in today's hectic corporate environment.

Setting standards

We need to know how well we are measuring up, and whether we should be changing anything. But unless we are clear about the standards we are aiming for and our targets, how can we possibly improve?

When learning to drive, most people are taught: MIRROR – SIGNAL – MANOEUVRE. This can be used in teamwork and leadership as well. If you want someone to change speed or direction then you need to help them.

Mirror

Where have you come from? What obstacles have you avoided? Who's following you? Who's trying to overtake you? But beware! What you see in a mirror is not real. It's only an interpretation, from one perspective.

Signal

How can you let other people know your intentions?
How far in advance of the change should you indicate?
How can you make sure they are paying attention to you?
How can you ensure that they understand your signals?

But beware! It's important to check that what you have signalled has been received and understood by others. Don't just assume, otherwise there could be 'accidents'.

Manoeuvre

How do you need to reposition yourself in relation to others? What kind of change will you be making? How will it affect others? What changes to speed and direction will you need to make? What are the rules about priorities? Are you confident in your skills, knowledge and attitudes in making the manoeuvre?

But beware! Make sure that other people 'on board' with you are also comfortable with what you are proposing, particularly if one of them is holding the 'map'.

Purchasing – good resources

Just as marathon runners need a range of different clothes, equipment and amenities to be successful, so your team members need certain tools, facilities and resources to carry out their work. It is equally important that all these different items should work well together.

Providing – good rest and refreshment

In a marathon, the organizers know they have to provide facilities to ensure the health and safety and general well-being of everyone involved. There will be, among other things, first-aid tents and drinks tables.

Health and safety are paramount. In an office environment, it could be tempting to think that accidents don't happen. But scissors, trailing flexes and open filing-cabinet drawers still account for a large number of days off sick each year. No doubt your organization will also have a smoking policy, but there should also be one that covers excessive drinking and the use of unauthorized drugs.

You need to be a caretaker – you must take good care of the members of your team. In conjunction with the health and safety adviser for your organization or section, you should undertake a risk assessment for your working area. Keep your people involved. Report all findings to senior management. Notify the trade unions and professional associations or institute. Monitor the situation regularly. Make sure it is brought to people's attention frequently. Keep it on the agenda at important meetings.

Ergonomic issues and matters of concern surrounding the continual use of computers – for example, potential problems with repetitive strain injury or the use of visual display units by pregnant women – must be constantly monitored. Your team will be grateful that you put their health and safety above all other considerations.

Partying – celebrating success

Your department may or may not have a highly developed sports and social culture, ranging from the formal – for example, squash league tables, fixtures and outings – to the informal – for example, after-work socializing, away-days and lunchtime gatherings.

You should do all you can to start or support such events, as in many ways they can provide the glue that helps to make the team stick together. An annual barbecue in your back garden can do wonders for team morale! And it's amazing the benefit to be gained from everyone spending the day together being pampered at a health spa!

You must also get into the habit of thanking people – individually for a good piece of work or collectively for a project delivered on time. Praise people in public, and make sure you are sincere. Award prizes and make gifts by all means, but don't embarrass your team with over-extravagant shows of gratitude. Often it can be a small but meaningful gesture that is remembered longest and appreciated most.

Make sure that other significant stakeholders know of your team's successes as well – both within and outside the organization. Team members will share the triumph and increasingly see themselves as a unit that pulls together to make even greater contributions and achieve even more.

'Good humour is a tonic for mind and body. It is the best antidote for anxiety and depression. It is a business asset. It attracts and keeps friends.'

– *Grenville Kleiser*

Many of us find it easy to slip into cynicism and sarcasm, finding fault with others or thinking of all the reasons why their ideas would never work.

POSITIVE THINKING FOR THE FUTURE

However, people need hope, because it is hope that banishes despair and overcomes stress. It holds open the door of opportunity for truth to enter.

'Wherever you see a successful business, someone once made a courageous decision.'

– Peter Drucker

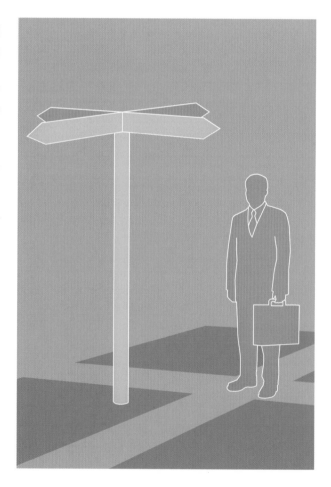

You need to boost people's confidence

People today are often unhappy at their work, or depressed by who they are, or saddened by what they've done. There are too many regrets. Perhaps some of your team members are struggling with feelings of rejection or low self-esteem.

Team leaders need to build people up, encourage them and support their efforts. All of this is central to 'transformational leadership'. It simply requires a future orientation in our outlook that is positive and optimistic. Far from being a vague, wishy-washy human resources fad, transformation is a bottom-line issue that is demonstrated not in platitudes and speeches but in powerful action.

As a leader, you should want the best for your team. They will depend on you to be sympathetic to their concerns and a good listener to their anxieties. But you will need to be constantly providing suggestions, options, alternatives and a range of possibilities. This will allow them to look outside of their normal and comfortable surroundings and everyday work. By helping them to remove their blinkered view, and by challenging their assumptions and stereotypes, you will let them find exciting new ways of solving their problems. This will promote a sense of confidence and success, which in turn will give them hope and a positive outlook.

Hope is vital for making possibilities become realities. It will enable both the team and its individual members to cope with the difficulties and problems that are bound to occur. It will also help to overcome the inevitable cynicism and sarcasm of those who feel jealous, fearful or threatened by proposed changes.

'It is amazing what can be accomplished when nobody cares about who gets the credit.'

– Robert Yates

You have probably heard the old saying that being an expert in any field is the result of 10 per cent inspiration and 90 per cent perspiration!

BREATHING NEW LIFE INTO YOUR TEAM

> 'Whenever an individual or a business decides that success has been attained, progress stops.'
>
> – Thomas Watson

This is sometimes said to encourage people to work hard and at other times to play down someone's extraordinary gifts or abilities. Either way, inspiration is crucial to the success of your role as a leader.

You need to inspire people

A number of writers have taken historical leaders – mostly from a military background – as models. This is not necessarily helpful for those of us working in modern service-driven organizations. Nevertheless, it would appear that most leaders of quality have the ability to inspire the people in their team.

Inspiration comprises three separate but integrated aspects: vision, purpose and motivation.

1 Vision

We are all very busy at work and are often snowed under by the pressures that come from having to meet deadlines, achieve targets and fulfil stakeholders' expectations. Life can seem very difficult and we sometimes cry out for a little breathing space. We are desperate for an opportunity to reflect, take stock, and think about what we're doing.

The strategic is often at the mercy of the operational. This explains why managers are often accused of not being able to see the wood for the trees!

It is essential that you, as a leader, model good practice. This will involve viewing the situation from different perspectives. First, look above, around and below. This is sometimes known as 'helicopter vision' and will give you a new perspective.

- Observe how the team appears from other people's points of view
- Stand back and look at how the work of your team fits in with that of other teams
- Consider the consequences of your actions on the efforts of other departments and organizations in the supply chain
- Watch where you've come from and where you're going
- Look out for obstacles in your way

Secondly, look beyond the immediate and the everyday. This is known as 'strategic vision'.

- Look over several departments' budgets, forecasts and actual outcomes
- Survey the departmental and organizational strategic plans
- Keep an eye on medium- and long-term goals as well as short-term imperatives
- Track developments by competitors, suppliers, customers and collaborators
- Commission pioneers and scouts to discover unexpected changes or problems ahead
- Invite new members into the team
- Encourage members to join other teams
- Project to some point in the future and then develop a plan to get your team from here to there, known as the creative vision

External forces for change

In order for you to make change rather than merely respond to it, you need to be able to plot developments in any of these forces for change:

- Political
- Economic
- Social
- Technological
- Legal
- Environmental

Political

Politics and government policies are changing all the time. As a leader, you must learn to see the wider picture with regard to what is happening at the local, regional and national level. Increasingly, you should also be on the lookout for changes at the continental and global level. In this way, you can spot changes at a time when you can still influence their impact on your organization.

However, politics also take place within your own organization. People are constantly forming groups and alliances in order to try to bend others to their own will. You should be very careful about playing games like this as they have a nasty habit of backfiring! Instead, be open about your purpose and direction, aim to inform and involve people, and strive for commitment and buy-in.

Economic

Changes to buying patterns and disposable income can be affected at a local level by variations in, say, house prices and at a national level by rates of inflation or unemployment or the government's borrowing limits. You cannot influence any of these, but you must be aware of the impact they could have on your organization and your team.

Increasingly, financial pressures and worries are affecting the amount of stress people are under at work. Therefore, work–life balance is an important consideration, and one you *can* do something about. Be willing to alter how and when your team members are at work.

Social

Society is changing all the time, and the rate of that change is increasing. For example: more people are living and working in cities or more people are saving less. You could add to the list with little difficulty.

As a team leader, it is your role to note these changes and anticipate their effects on the performance of your team. People's eating and smoking habits, abuse of alcohol and drugs, different patterns and fashions in dress – all these will affect how people work together.

Technological

Everybody is aware of the speed with which new gadgets are advertised on television and in newspapers, and then appear in the shops. More importantly, the use of technology dramatically affects the ways in which we work. But don't let the potential power· and effectiveness of, say, e-mail destroy the working atmosphere or relationships by cutting down on face -to-face interactions.

It is also worth remembering that all sophisticated technology requires electricity. Could your team continue working if there was a power cut?

Legal

Legislation is becoming more prolific and also encouraging greater centralization of power. Litigation is increasing at an alarming rate as well. When people are unable or unwilling to take responsibility for themselves and others, with a sense of community and mutual support, then a 'blame' culture will prevail.

In a number of organizations, the human resources department's main role is to deal with problems with employment tribunals. As a leader, your task is to encourage your team to look after itself and its members. Instead of complaining, finding fault or seeking recrimination, you need to set an example by always working to a higher ethical and moral standard. Corporate social responsibility will be increasingly important in the future.

Environmental

Green issues are at the forefront of a lot of people's minds these days. It is highly likely that some in your team will view such matters as extremely important. You need to be aware of what your organization is doing to address considerations such as these in relation to its products and services, the ergonomics and physical location of its buildings, and its use of fuel and energy.

People in your team may want to raise funds through sponsored events, to encourage charitable donations or to increase the organization's contact with and influence

'It is change, continuing change, inevitable change, that is the dominant factor in society today. No sensible decision can be made any longer without taking into account not only the world as it is but as it will be.'

– Isaac Asimov

> 'In order to have a winner, the team must have a feeling of unity; every person must put the team first – ahead of personal glory.'
>
> *– Paul Bryant*

in the community. You will find all of these excellent ways of cementing relationships, since they deal directly with people's values, principles and attitudes.

Internal forces for change

• Meaning
• Openness
• Relationships
• Trust
• Attitudes
• Respect

Meaning

The reasoning behind senior managers' organizational decisions and actions is becoming more significant for the working population. It is not so easy for them merely to impose change from the top without consulting employees.

When people understand why they are doing a job:

• They will be more interested in their own – and other people's – work
• They will be more motivated to do a good job
• They will be more aware of others around them
• They will perform more efficiently and effectively
• They will produce work of a higher quality

During the Second World War, a prisoner called Viktor Frankl, who was being persecuted, finally had nothing left, not even his clothes. However, he managed to retain his dignity and his hold on life by looking for meaning in everything that happened to him. Once he found purpose and a rationale, he was even able to say to his captors, 'You can take away everything I have except my choice to love you.' From this he developed a theory of logotherapy, which essentially enables people to find meaning in life.

As a leader, you must ask your team members questions rather than giving them directions. Then you will be in a better position to understand their differing motivations and to work out what is meaningful for each of them. You must also include them in all consultations and decisions affecting the team, so that they can find meaning in what they do.

Openness

There are many things that will affect the degree of openness that exists between the people in your team. For example:

• Personalities
• Background and experiences
• Traditions and way of life
• Organizational culture
• Management styles
• Office layout
• Stress and tensions caused through deadlines and scarce resources
• Competition – both internal and external

In addition, some people will be more reserved because of previous hurts. And once they feel betrayed, it will usually take a long time to earn their trust and respect again.

The best way to encourage openness is to model it yourself. This will mean that you become quite vulnerable, so make sure you have a good support network outside work!

You will be surprised how quickly people around you start to become honest about themselves. They will trust you with quite personal details about themselves. Once you show your own willingness to be seen as a normal human being who makes mistakes, they will follow suit.

Relationships

Depending on the size and structure of your team, and he length of time different people have been members of it, there will be a wide variety of relationships at play. To a certain extent we all behave differently at different times, depending on who we're with, so you will need to make it easy for people to relate in their own ways with each other. However, your role as a leader is also to be available to help people whenever misunderstandings develop.

> '**People have been known to achieve more as a result of working with others than against them.**'
>
> – *Allan Fromme*

Trust

Fundamentally, since we are social beings, we need to work with other people. Relationships are built on trust, on a willingness to depend on others. We have faith that the person who has promised to do something will keep their word. But trust is also about valuing someone enough to give them something important of ourselves – whether it's a confidential piece of information or a special kind of project that shows we can rely on them to carry it out on their own.

Trust shows that you have confidence in someone. It can take a long time to build, a split second to destroy and even longer to rebuild again.

One of the quickest ways to destroy trust is through gossip. Therefore, as a leader, don't allow the organizational grapevine to flourish. Instead, constantly be on the lookout for new ways to communicate – at all levels – that do away with the need to gossip.

Attitudes

Everyone gets moody at times and we certainly all have a range of opinions about different things. But attitudes can be said to be mostly about people, not things. They are a function of beliefs and values.

In the workplace, it's not appropriate to try to change someone's beliefs but their values are always open to be altered. This often happens on training courses, particularly in relation to the organization's products or services. Consequently employees' attitudes can be affected as well. Once you affect their values, their attitudes will change.

Respect

Respect is all about how we treat those with whom we come into contact and encompasses questions of dignity, rapport and esteem. It is also to do with the extent to which we look down on other people and whether we are sensitive to their feelings.

The abuse of power at work is probably one of the last taboo areas, rarely discussed in polite circles. Once the door of his office is closed, the manager is all-powerful and can ask an employee to do almost anything – and that person will usually oblige! Unfortunately, some managers have abused this sort of power. We have all heard stories of awful things being done in the name of business! You need to focus instead on the huge amount of good that can come from such a powerful relationship being channelled towards the good of the team and the organization.

Let's hold in mind an adaptation of just part of the model of personal relationships that is based on the PARENT–ADULT–CHILD notion of transactional analysis. Put very simply, and just to restrict it to the work situation for our purposes, the model proposes that there can be a wide variety of relationships between leaders and team members. Let us have a look at just one typical application.

If workers feel that their manager is adopting a patronizing, supercilious, arrogant approach and undermining their integrity by appearing all-knowing and condescending, then they can easily become angry, antagonistic or openly aggressive. This can then easily descend into what is known as an 'attack/defend' spiral, where nobody wins.

As the leader, you must take the initiative and be the first to change. You need to adopt a much more 'adult' style of approach: in other words, listen more, treat team members as equals and respect their contributions. It is very difficult under these circumstances for employees to remain in 'parent' mode and so they usually follow you by taking a more 'adult' approach themselves.

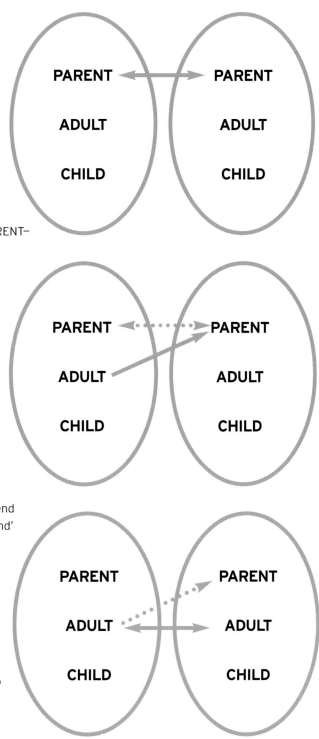

2 Purpose

Based on the experience of a great many people, it has been found that employees are willing to undertake almost anything at work if they know the reason *why*. The purpose of a task, a job or a function is possibly more important than the process or even the product.

If you, as team leader, tell someone they have to do something, they might well do it, albeit reluctantly. But if they make a mistake, have an accident or encounter an unforeseen difficulty, they won't know what caused it, how to overcome it or how to prevent it happening again.

However, if you explain the background to your request and the purpose of the assignment, they will understand your reasoning. They will then be able to see the context and the overall intention. And if they can go on to imagine the possible consequences, they will grasp the significance and importance of the job in hand.

Equally necessary is for you to show determination and perseverance. Your team members will expect to see in you a significant degree of courage, willpower and strength of mind. If this is the case, then they will be more than happy to follow you wherever you lead them, because they will have put their faith in you and will stay with you, no matter what complications you may come across.

3 Motivation

Different people are motivated by different things. Most of us work for money − in other words, extrinsic motivation. However, we much prefer going out to work, so there must be a number of additional − intrinsic − benefits that we need and look for in the working environment.

Use the form opposite to find out what motivates you. Then complete the same form for each member of your team. How easy was it to do? How well do you really know them? Finally get everybody in the team to do the same exercise, firstly for themselves and then for each other. How closely do they match? Be open and positive and discuss with the team what you have found. Decide what you can now change.

WHAT IS YOUR MOTIVATION?

Tick all the motives that apply to you/your team:

YOU	TICK ✓
Being part of a group	
Opportunity to do a good job	
Knowledge of success	
Prospects for creativity and innovation	
Security and support in regular activity	
Sense of personal responsibility	
Chance to develop	
Chance to save for something special	

YOUR TEAM	TICK ✓
Being part of a group	
Opportunity to do a good job	
Knowledge of success	
Prospects for creativity and innovation	
Security and support in regular activity	
Sense of personal responsibility	
Chance to develop	
Chance to save for something special	

A little appreciation goes an awfully long way, although it is certainly the case that insincerity and faint praise do more harm than good.

SAYING 'THANK YOU'

So let's see if we can tease out some of the elements of this very important aspect of leadership.

You need to be appreciative

Most of us at work are very happy to continue what we've been doing for some time. We don't expect plaudits and would probably be embarrassed to be singled out for a public display of affirmation every other day. We know that promotions, bonuses and pay rises are most unlikely to be offered as a reward for hard work. But wouldn't it be nice once in a while to have our efforts acknowledged?

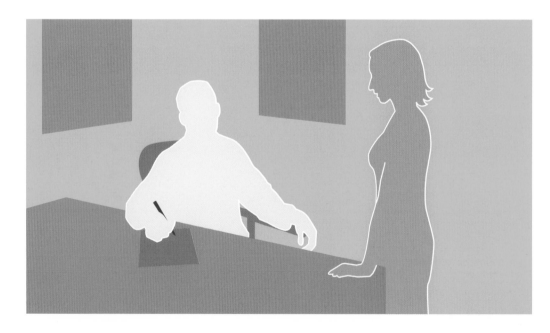

More importantly, many people are 'flying blind' in the working environment. They just don't know if they are doing what is expected. Unless the boss is shouting at them and until the next ambiguous or unhelpful appraisal, most people assume they're doing OK – but they just don't know.

Generally speaking, most people in the workplace share a desire to receive praise, though they might list a number of different reasons. For example:

- Pleasure
- Recognition
- Advancement
- Interest
- Security
- Encouragement

Knowledge of results is fundamental to performance improvement.

Pleasure

Even though at times all of us are required to perform tasks which are boring or mundane, work should on the whole be enjoyable. Unless the people in your team actually get more pleasure than not from coming to work, and can see some benefit in giving their labour to the organization, then they are unlikely to stay very long. As a leader, there are a number of things you could consider doing to increase people's pleasure at being part of your team.

You must take every opportunity to speak on your team's behalf about:

- Management arrangements
- The effect of organizational policies, practices, plans and priorities
- Interpersonal relationships

> '**To cultivate kindness is a valuable part of the business of life.**'
>
> – *Samuel Johnson*

You should also be involved in championing their cause and putting forward their case for increased and/or improved:

- Salary
- Job security
- Working conditions

In addition, when you show your interest in them as individuals, they will take pleasure from knowing that you do not see them just as members of a team. They all have outside influences and pressures – whether it's caring for dependants, moving home or saving for a special holiday. Feeling that they are valued and that what they do is important, they will gain pleasure from contributing to the team and its successes.

And have fun! Deliberately make time for doughnuts, dressing-down days, fun-runs or farewell drinks.

Recognition

Each of us is unique, but so often we are not treated as such. The forms and databases we are asked to complete all too often don't provide space or opportunity for us to give real or appropriate responses. Sometimes, we're not even referred to by name and a job title or work number is used instead, further compounding our sense of anonymity.

So take time to treat people differently. Now that equal opportunities should be regarded as normal, make sure that you don't treat everybody the same! Ensure that you respect people's differences and respond accordingly. Acknowledge that their distinctive characteristics can benefit you and the team. Avoid cloning at all costs! Creativity and originality can only add to your team's quality and performance.

People want to be noticed, so take notice of them. You will soon become aware of how they behave towards you and towards each other. Don't jump just because they ask you to. And don't ignore them either just because they're quiet.

You should be determined to discover their strengths and weaknesses. Then you can play to their strengths and provide training in their weaker areas. Give them opportunities to contribute and excel. Introduce, include and involve them whenever appropriate. Defend, protect and shield them whenever necessary.

So, recognition involves:

- **Giving and receiving peer respect**
- **Self-assessment of a job's worth**
- **Acknowledgement of a job well done**

Advancement

People are realistic and don't expect promotion to positions of responsibility all the time. In fact, with the number of organizational exercises for downsizing, delayering and re-engineering that have taken place, opportunities for this kind of advancement are limited.

Instead, as their leader, you should be constantly on the lookout for ways to offer your team members job enrichment, job development and job enlargement.

Essentially, this could include:

- **Different work**
- **More important work**
- **Harder work**

There are a number of techniques to help you in this. For example:

- **Delegation/empowerment**
- **Secondments/attachments**
- **Assignments/projects**
- **Presentations/reports**
- **Visits/conferences**
- **Shadowing/mentoring**
- **Coaching/job instruction**

Interest

Your work colleagues and associates generally want a degree of variety in their work. They are looking for a healthy amount of mental stimulation, together with opportunities to make decisions. They look to you to provide means for them to use a range of skills.

If the work becomes too repetitive and predictable, then their powers of concentration and insight may diminish. Once they give less attention to what they are doing, then standards will inevitably fall.

But as soon as you find ways of increasing the sorts of duties required of them, then their output will almost certainly increase, both quantitatively and qualitatively. Clearly, there must be a sensible balance between old and new duties: too great a change is never good and too much difference will only confuse.

Therefore, as a leader, you should consider the following two techniques:

- **Multi-skilling**
- **Job rotation**

Multi-skilling is a method for enabling individuals to take on aspects of a task greater than their current responsibilities. So, for example, if they are normally used to carrying out the duties of a television cameraman, then, by introducing them to the latest technology, you could help them take on the role of sound engineer and lighting technician as well.

To take a more mundane example, if they are used to arranging for job advertisements to be placed in appropriate publications, then you could provide training and opportunities for them to also write the relevant job descriptions and person specifications.

By contrast, job rotation is for helping two or more team members to take on new work. Either they can do a direct job swap, by carrying out each other's duties, or they can pass across part of their work. Alternatively, several people can swap roles. It can be helpful for them to actually change desks and machines as relevant.

To give an example, when graduates are first recruited in some organizations, they are appointed to an integrated development scheme. In addition to formal training programmes and professional education courses, they will be attached to a specific department, section or unit for a given period of time, such as six months. During that time, they will carry out a range of duties and undertake particular projects, sometimes in conjunction with their studies. They are often required to write and present a report to managers at the end of their attachment, outlining their accomplishments. Subsequently, they will move to a new area, as will all the others recruited at the same time. Eventually, after a couple of years or so, both the graduates and the organization will be in a much better position to decide on an appropriate career path.

Security

Even when the economy is not in recession, when interest rates and unemployment are low, people have a basic need for job security. Those who are self-employed often prefer to have at least one or two major clients they can count on to give them a significant amount of work and income. The main fear of many, both self-employed and employed, is not having sufficient income to pay the bills at home. Worrying about the possibility of redundancy can be paralyzing.

But there is more to it than that. Unemployment and redundancy have been shown to destroy people's sense of self-worth, dignity and esteem. In Western capitalist economies our identity is closely linked with our occupation, so not having a job can be perceived as very problematic for many individuals and their dependants. With it come fear, shame or blame; fear of losing possessions or space; and fear of inability or incompetence.

As a team leader, you may not be able to exert great influence on the strategic changes that take place at the organizational level. However, you can affect how your team members are viewed when it comes to decisions about redeployment, outsourcing and retirement. Within your grasp are openings to increase their *employability*.

Ask yourself – and them – on a fairly regular basis how you can extend the range of their knowledge, skills and attitudes. Look for creative methods of combining their abilities in new and dynamic permutations. Find ways to use their dormant or latent talents developed in previous jobs or in their social and leisure activities. Use innovative methods to demonstrate to as many people as possible the importance of their contribution to the team's performance and the wider organization's output and success.

Encouragement

You have a major role to play in giving support to your people in times of crisis. You should try to find alternative ways to help them with their complications. Don't attempt to take their problems away from them, but assist them in dealing with their struggles and finding solutions for themselves.

Problem-solving and decision-making are two very important skills that you should develop, first for yourself and then for your team.

This will help to expand and extend their abilities in coping when you're not around. It will also help them to transfer their learning and to apply their knowledge generically to new situations.

A no-blame, low-risk culture is necessary for them to really believe that risk-taking is something to be admired and that mistake-making is not likely to be judged as a career-limiting activity.

You must be there for them. Don't try to play the amateur psychiatrist, but reassure the people in your team. Help them to see the big picture. Aid them in their search for meaning. Instil confidence in them again by reminding them of their strengths. Above all, show them – and tell them – that your acceptance of them as individuals is not determined purely by their performance.

Many years ago, a young man was taking part in an outdoor development course. He tried many activities for the first time, including caving, potholing and canoeing. But for him, the most daunting exercise of all was rock climbing. He disqualified himself with phrases such as 'I've never done this before', 'I'm no good at this kind of thing', and 'I'm really not that interested in it anyway'. The instructors quickly identified the fear that was preventing him from taking on this new challenge. And so, for over half an hour, one of the leaders showed him exactly where to put his feet, how to hold on, and which rope to use. Climbing right next to him, the expert constantly encouraged him, declaring his belief in him, and sharing his determination to get to the top. He reached the summit. It was one of the young man's most exhilarating achievements.

'Leadership is a matter of having people look at you and gaining confidence, seeing how you react. If you are in control, they're in control.'

– *Tom Landry*

Lack of leadership may cause a team or an organization to fail. Often leaders believe they are providing good leadership when in fact they are not.

LEADERSHIP EXERCISES

What kind of leadership do you provide?

Read the statements on page 111 and rate each on the scale below as to whether they are true where you work:

1 = not true
2 = rarely true
3 = sometimes true
4 = often true
5 = always true

0	60	95

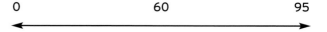

Scoring and interpretation

Total your responses and place the number on the line above.

If you scored less than 60 You are probably experiencing good leadership where you work. You are most likely satisfied with your work situation and the way work is done in your organization.

If you scored 60 or above People are experiencing the problems that accompany lack of strong leadership. The higher your score, the more challenges you encounter each day at work. Stronger leadership would eliminate many of the problems you and your colleagues experience.

	STATEMENT	POINTS
1	Workers make no suggestions for improvements.	
2	There are battles over resources and assignments.	
3	There are complaints after meetings about issues not discussed in the meetings.	
4	Workers have no pride in the organization or their work.	
5	Relationships between colleagues are strained.	
6	'Us versus them' talk is often heard.	
7	Workers are unwilling to take responsibility for their mistakes.	
8	Workers' grievances about managers are increasing.	
9	People are complaining more about their working conditions.	
10	People are increasingly missing deadlines.	
11	There appears to be an increase in unethical behaviour.	
12	The 'idea of the month' to fix things is a joke.	
13	Workers appear to want more information from their managers.	
14	Employees are asking for more involvement in decision-making.	
15	It is increasingly difficult to find new, talented workers.	
16	Staff do not take on leadership roles, even when the opportunity presents itself.	
17	High-performing recruits are leaving to work elsewhere.	
18	Rumours and the grapevine are widespread.	
19	People act as though their projects are a waste of time.	
	TOTAL	

Select your leadership style

For each section in the chart below, place a 1 next to the statement that best describes you. Place a 2 beside your second choice.

INFLUENCE

(C)   I belong to several groups but only attend when something especially interests me.

(D)   I like to work on committees but don't like to be the chairperson.

(A)   I lose interest in groups when they go along in the same old rut and don't listen to my suggestions.

(B)   I consciously seek, and obtain, leadership in many of my groups' activities.

(E)   I am often selected as leader of groups without seeking it.

TACT

(A)   People frequently misunderstand my comments.

(C)   My acquaintances tell me that I am noted for handling many difficult situations without arousing ill-will.

(D)   People seldom resent it when I must correct what they are doing or must criticize them.

(E)   I consciously study how to handle people tactfully.

(B)   Before I try to get others to accept my point of view, I first try to find out how they feel so that I can adapt my ideas to theirs.

COMMUNICATION

(E)   I always assume the other person will be friendly and take the initiative in meeting them more than halfway.

(D)   People tell me they come to me with problems they wouldn't even discuss with their own families.

(B)   I always try to give the other person some incentive or some reason for doing what I want done.

(C)   When a conversation lags at a party of strangers, I try to fill in the silence by finding a topic of general interest.

(A)   I have definite ideas about the failings of others and don't hesitate to express them.

MATURITY

(A)   I want what I want when I want it, regardless of the consequences for myself or others.

(E)   I frequently let others have the last word.

(D)   I have been told that I can take well-meant, constructive criticism graciously.

(B)   I believe in telling others the truth if it is for their own good.

(C)   I take a stand on issues in which I believe, after looking into the pros and cons, even if they are unpopular

ATTITUDES

(A)   I get annoyed when people don't do things my way and sometimes my temper gets the best of me.

(B)   I try to show the attitude to another person that I would want them to show to me.

(E)   I believe I should make every effort to accept change and try to keep changing with the times.

(D)   I patiently listen to people with whom I disagree.

(C)   I am indecisive when it comes to making a decision; sometimes I wait so long circumstances force a decision upon me.

COOPERATION

(D)   When people have a misunderstanding, I try to intervene and reconcile them.

(C)   In dealing with others, I try to put myself in their shoes and act towards them the way I'd like them to act towards me.

(E)   I am willing to accept the help of others, provided it does not interfere with their work.

(A)   When I want information from others, I feel I have a right to demand it because I am acting on behalf of my boss.

(B)   If my boss says to me, 'Tell so-and-so I want this right away,' I change both the message and voice tone to, 'The boss would appreciate this as soon as possible.'

	1ST CHOICE (1s)	2ND CHOICE (2s)	TOTAL
As			
Bs			
Cs			
Ds			
Es			

Scoring and interpretation

Each statement you chose has a letter in the left-hand column. Use the chart above to make two lists of the 1s and 2s you marked against the statements. Note your totals in the right-hand column. The letters each correspond with the following leadership styles:

A Authoritative
B Political
C Evaluative
D Democratic
E Laissez-faire

Authoritative

This approach is one in which the leader retains as much power and decision-making authority as possible. The leader does not consult employees, nor are they allowed to give any input. Workers are expected to obey orders without any explanations. Motivation is produced by creating a structured set of rewards and punishments.

Political

Political leadership is where the leader leads 'by the book'. Everything must be done according to procedure or policy. If it isn't covered by the rule book, the leader refers to the next level above. This leader is really more of a police officer than a leader. They are there to enforce the rules.

Evaluative

Evaluative leadership is seen where the leader spends time weighing up all the benefits and drawbacks of a situation before making a decision or committing his team to a course of action. They are often governed by fear. Occasionally, this can result in a lack of determination or perseverance. In extremes, it produces paralysis or intransigence.

Democratic

This leadership style is also called the participative style as it encourages team workers to be a part of the decision making. The democratic leader keeps their team informed about everything that affects their work and shares with them the decision making and problem solving responsibilities. It requires the leader to be a coach who has the final say, but gathers information before making a decision. Democratic leadership can produce high quality and high quantity work for long periods of time. Many people like the trust they receive and respond with cooperation and high morale.

Laissez-faire

The laissez-faire leadership style is also known as the 'hands-off' style. It is one in which the leader provides little or no direction and gives members as much freedom as possible. All authority or power is given to the employees and they must determine goals, make decisions, and resolve problems on their own.

Varying your leadership style

While some argue that an appropriate leadership style may depend on the particular situation, there are three other factors that always influence which leadership style to use:

The leader What personality, knowledge, values, ethics, and experiences does the leader have? What do they think will work?

The team Workers are individuals with different personalities and backgrounds. The leadership style used will vary depending upon the individual employee and what they will respond to.

The organization The traditions, values, philosophy, and concerns of the organization will influence how a leader acts.

Leadership methods quiz

It is often said that the best leaders are those who can vary their approach to leadership in a variety of situations. This quiz will help you to understand your main approach to leadership, and then to choose some alternatives depending on the circumstances, the team, the organizational culture, and the priorities.

The table opposite shows a list of statements about leadership behaviour. Read each one carefully, then, using the following scale, decide the extent to which it actually applies to you. For best results, answer as truthfully as possible.

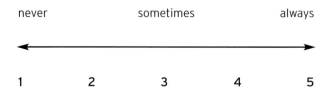

never		sometimes		always
1	2	3	4	5

	STATEMENT	POINTS
1	I encourage my team to participate when it comes to decision-making and I try to implement their ideas and suggestions.	
2	Nothing is more important than accomplishing a goal or task.	
3	I closely monitor a plan to ensure a task or project will be completed in time.	
4	I enjoy coaching people on new tasks and procedures.	
5	The more challenging a task is, the more I enjoy it.	
6	I encourage my staff to be creative about their jobs.	
7	When seeing a complex task through to completion I ensure that every detail is accounted for.	
8	I find it easy to carry out several complicated tasks at once.	
9	I enjoy reading articles and books about training, leadership and psychology and then putting what I have read into action.	
10	When correcting mistakes, I do not worry about jeopardizing relationships.	
11	I manage my time efficiently.	
12	I enjoy explaining the intricacies and details of a complex task or project to my team.	
13	Breaking large projects into small tasks is second nature to me.	
14	Nothing is more important than building a great team.	
15	I enjoy analysing problems.	
16	I honour other people's boundaries.	
17	Counselling my staff to improve their performance is natural for me.	
18	I enjoy reading articles and then implementing the new procedures I have learned.	

PEOPLE			TASK		
STATEMENT	POINTS		STATEMENT	POINTS	
1			2		
4			3		
6			5		
9			7		
10			8		
12			11		
14			13		
16			15		
17			18		
TOTAL			TOTAL		
TOTAL X 0.2			TOTAL X 0.2		

Scoring

Transfer your answers to the chart above. Add the score in each column and multiply its total by 0.2. For example, in the first column (People), if you answered 5, 3, 4, 4, 3, 2, 5, 4 ,3 then your final score is 33 x 0.2 = 6.6.

Transferring your score to the matrix

Plot your final People and Task scores on the graph opposite by drawing a horizontal line from the approximate People score (on the vertical axis) to the right of the matrix, and drawing a vertical line from approximate Task score (on the horizontal axis) to the top of the matrix.

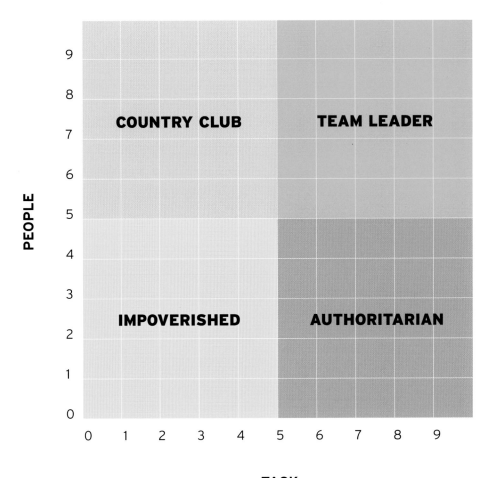

PEOPLE

9
8
7 COUNTRY CLUB   TEAM LEADER
6
5
4
3
2 IMPOVERISHED   AUTHORITARIAN
1
0

0   1   2   3   4   5   6   7   8   9

TASK

The results

The leadership method that you are most comfortable with is revealed by the area where the two lines intersect. This will give you an idea of your leadership style, but, like any other instrument that attempts to profile a person, you have to take other factors into account. For example, does your organization and staff rate you as a leader? Do you get the job done? Do you take care of your staff? You should review the statements on page 117 and reflect on any low scores by asking yourself, 'If I scored higher in that area, would I be a more effective leader?' And if the answer is yes, then it should become a personal action item.

Authoritarian

This leadership method can be effective when:

- New, untrained employees do not know which tasks to perform or which procedures to follow
- Effective supervision can be provided only through detailed orders and instructions
- Employees do not respond to any other leadership style
- There are high-volume production needs on a daily basis
- There is limited time in which to make a decision
- Your power is challenged by an employee
- The area was poorly managed
- Work needs to be coordinated with another department or organization

This method should not be used when:

- Employees become tense, fearful or resentful
- Employees expect to have their opinions heard
- Employees begin depending on their manager to make all their decisions
- There is low employee morale, high turnover, absenteeism and work stoppage

Country club

This leadership method can be effective when:

- Employees are performing routine tasks over and over
- Employees need to understand certain standards or procedures
- Employees are working with dangerous or delicate equipment that requires a definite set of procedures to operate
- Safety or security training is being conducted
- Employees are performing tasks that require handling cash

This method should not be used when:

- Work habits form that are hard to break, especially if they are no longer useful
- Employees lose their interest in their jobs and in their fellow workers
- Employees only do what is expected of them

Team leader

This leadership method is most effective when:

- You want to keep employees informed about matters that affect them
- You want employees to share in decision-making and problem-solving duties
- You want to provide opportunities for employees to develop a high sense of personal growth and job satisfaction
- There is a large or complex problem that requires lots of input to solve
- Changes must be made or problems solved that affect employees or groups of employees
- You want to encourage team building and participation

This method should not be used when:

- There is not enough time to get everyone's input
- It is easier and more cost-effective for you to make the decision
- The business can't afford mistakes
- You feel threatened by this type of leadership
- Employee safety is a critical concern

Impoverished

This leadership method is most effective when:

- Employees are highly skilled, experienced and educated
- Employees have pride in their work and the drive to do it successfully on their own
- Outside experts, such as staff specialists or consultants are being used
- Employees are trustworthy and experienced

This method should not be used when:

- It makes employees feel insecure at the unavailability of a manager
- You cannot provide regular feedback to let employees know how well they are doing
- You are unable to thank employees for their good work
- You don't understand your responsibilities and hope your employees can cover for you

Well, we've got to the end. So how was it for you? It would be good to spend a few moments now reflecting on what you have learned.

SUMMARY

1 For me, creating my team means

2 Teamworking involves

3 Building relationships is all about

4 Building trust entails

5 Building commitment is a way of

6 Building success is achieved through

7 Pulling together helps people to

8 Gathering resources indicates

9 Sharing and caring shows that

10 Contributing understanding is done by

11 Celebrating differences demonstrates

12 Getting it together is exhibited by

13 Aiming high signifies

14 Teamworking exercises helped me to learn that

15 For me, leading my team means

16 Leadership involves

17 Empowering my people shows that

18 Boosting a team is carried out by

19 Facilitate learning through

20 Encourage progress with

21 Give it all away by

22 Support and strengthen as a result of

23 Look beyond the immediate in order to

24 Positive thinking for the future requires

25 Breathe new life so that

26 Say 'thank you' in order that

27 The leadership exercises helped me to realize that

And since learning is never fully achieved until you do something with it, change what you are currently doing or tell someone about it ... go and talk to someone right now about what you have just written!

In conclusion

You must now draw up an action plan in order to decide what you are going to do with all your hard-won learning.

   You could ask yourself the following questions:

What am I going to do?
When will I complete it?
What help and resources will I need?
How will I measure my success?

   Finally, teamwork and leadership are not just fascinating things to learn about. They can actually become a way of life for you.

   Don't stop growing, maturing and developing – it's called lifelong learning.

   And why not pass on your newly acquired knowledge, skills and attitudes to another team leader just like yourself?

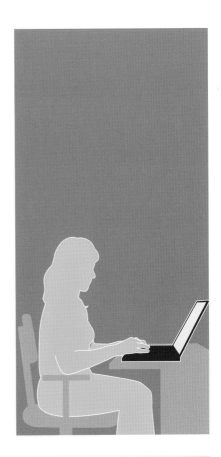

INDEX